THE FELLOWSHIP OF
THE MYSTERY

BEING THE BISHOP PADDOCK LECTURES DELIVERED
AT THE GENERAL THEOLOGICAL SEMINARY
NEW YORK, DURING LENT 1913

BY

JOHN NEVILLE FIGGIS

LITT. D., HON. D.D. (GLASGOW)

OF THE COMMUNITY OF THE RESURRECTION
HONORARY FELLOW OF ST. CATHARINE'S COLLEGE, CAMBRIDGE

SECOND IMPRESSION

LONGMANS, GREEN AND CO.
39 PATERNOSTER ROW, LONDON
FOURTH AVENUE & 30TH STREET, NEW YORK
BOMBAY, CALCUTTA, AND MADRAS

1915

THE FELLOWSHIP OF THE MYSTERY

TO

PHILIP MERCER RHINELANDER

D.D., D.C.L., LL.D.

BISHOP OF PENNSYLVANIA

IN GRATITUDE AND FRIENDSHIP

PREFACE

WITH slight changes, these lectures are
printed as they were delivered. Two Appendices are added which may further
elucidate the topics discussed. That on
John Henry Newman is reprinted from the
English Church Review. It appeared there
on the publication of Mr. Wilfrid Ward's
Life of Newman; and I have to thank the
Editor for kind permission to reprint it.
Since I have made allusion in the lectures
to Newman's theory of the ethics of conformity, it seemed not impertinent to add
this more elaborate appreciation of the
greatest of nineteenth-century apologists.

The other appendix on "Modernity *versus*
Modernism" deals with certain aspects of
the subject that have come into promi-
nence in the wake of the Kikuyu controversy. The war of pamphlets that preceded
and followed the unanimous declaration of
the Bishops of the Province of Canterbury
bore too close a relation to matters touched
upon in the text for me to leave the topic

unnoticed. The title of the appendix indicates its standpoint. I do not believe that the purely intellectualist standpoint in criticism is truly modern; and I am persuaded that it does not make good history. In the closing pages of the appendix I try to make it clear that it is not on matters of detail that we are at issue. We feel that the liberal school, in its most outstanding representatives, betrays a lack of insight into its own presuppositions and those of any real religion, as distinct from a philosophy. Controversy between the two parties is not likely to be serviceable, so long as the protagonists of liberalism can see nothing in their opponents but ignorance and stupidity. If they could realise that for us there is a certain quality in the Catholic religion which they appear to ignore, some progress might be possible.

Such progress in mutual understanding is becoming every day more real between the two parties commonly called Catholic and Evangelical. All do not recognise this; and not all who recognise it like the *rapprochement*. But the pressure of a common danger unites them; and each is beginning to recognise in the other the vital sense of faith in the Cross of Christ. Even

to an ultramontane the sacrifice of the mass
means the more secure realisation and
presentment before God of that atoning
work which inspires the Methodist to joy.
The advanced wing of the negative school
has begun to blame in Luther the retention
of the fundamental faith of Catholic Christianity. Many old antagonisms are dying
down. Vital Christianity draws people
together, as against merely conventional
religion on the one hand and the definite
anti-Christian adversary on the other. Let
us all use what means there are of drawing nearer, without sacrificing principle.
The writer would not knowingly, in either
this or any other book, speak in any terms
but those of affectionate reverence of that
Evangelical piety which is to him hallowed
by every sacred memory. This need not
mean but that we ought to fill out the
system by developing its implications and by
bringing it into closer relation with the sacramental and institutional sides of religion.

This need is the more patent, now that
antichrist is being revealed. The new
Teutonic Christianity discussed in the second
lecture is conducting its first mission—with
the bonfire of Louvain for its Bethlehem
star. Perhaps we shall hear less than we did

of the revised and Nietzscheanized edition of the Gospel proclaimed by Mr. Houston Stewart Chamberlain.[1] Since the Kaiser presented his work on the "Foundations of the Nineteenth Century" to all his officers, we have witnessed its outcome in the ruins of Rheims—a result by no means out of harmony with the author's attitude towards that Latin Catholicism of which Rheims was a supreme symbol. It must be borne in mind that it is this combination of a nominal Christianity with a Nietzschean moral that now dominates Germany. Those may be right who tell us that the direct disciples of Nietzsche are not our adversaries;—although even this is doubtful. At least Nietzsche had no extravagant belief in German culture. Doubtless he would turn in his grave at the thought of Prussian Junkerdom posing as the Superman; although we must bear in mind his other statement that the doctrine of the "Will to Power" was awakened in his mind by the sight of Prussian cavalry in 1870. Yet for all that, Nietzsche has done more than even Treitschke to produce the moral atmosphere which now pervades the German race

[1] Two illuminating articles by the editor in *The Interpreter* for April and July 1913 give a good account of this book.

—its worship of blind force, its contempt for all humane ideals, its goal of a conquering, full-blooded but disciplined aristocracy, governing with ruthless selfishness the vast mass of men, the herd of slave-races. For the "immoralism" of Nietzsche is a fact. Many deductions may be made. He had the poetic temperament; he loved to stimulate by paradox. He shows here and there a certain awe of the figure of Christ. He revolted against certain sentimentalism. He was a necessary reaction against Schopenhauer as well as against the mere passivism of Tolstoi. He had a sense of freedom, of beauty, of the need and value of heroism, of the need to sacrifice for a far future; he saw that the world wants redemption. He misunderstood Christian ethics, which is in the truest sense a yea-saying to the claims of life no less real and far more thoroughgoing than his own. If he had understood it, he might have been less hostile. He was not an intellectualist, but in open revolt against rationalism; and he had a contempt for all merely second-hand culture. To that extent, those are right who declare that professorial Germany is not inspired by Nietzsche. What is the truth is that he definitely heralded the reign of antichrist, if his principles were to be victorious. We need not discuss here his absolute rejection of otherworldly ideals in that cry "God is dead, God is dead" which rings through *Zarathrustra*. Such repudiation is possible, as Positivism has shown, by men who retain, in human relations, ideals which are by implication Christian—*i.e.* the worth of every man, the ideal of love. These ideals were definitely scorned by Nietzsche—except in two respects. His coming race of Super-men might show something of mutual sympathy towards each other; and the Christian morality—*i.e.* the slave-morality —might still be inculcated as the best way of keeping "the herd" in subjection to its lords. But Nietzsche's deliberate adoption of Napoleon as a near approach to what he wanted bears its ineffaceable mark on all that he writes. No amount of watering down can affect the fact that he repudiated not merely ecclesiastical Christianity, but the Christ himself, even as a human teacher. Yet he is a noble foe; and the charm of his writing wins even his adversaries. Nietzsche was a free spirit, as he claimed, turned the wrong way. In one sense, there would be more hope of him, than of Protestant "reducers" in their liberal sentimentalism, of which the result is apparent in a recent German manifesto.

Nothing has occurred which does not warrant the writer's assertion some time ago that the real danger now is in Nietzsche and his congeners. The fact that Nietzsche shares with Christians their faith in faith, in adventure, in joy through suffering, in the need of redemption, in the newness of the world, should guide us better as to the nature of our task. No longer for the most part shall we be faced with men who cannot believe the Christian Faith but wish they could. Rather our true adversaries will be those before whom many of the old difficulties mean nothing, but who oppose Christianity because they hate it. That is why modernism, as a purely intellectualist system, is not dangerous. It may undermine some beliefs, and do good to the orthodox, if it makes them attend to criticism. But the future is not with a Unitarianized Christianity. Professor Moll's egregious discovery that all the German misdeeds in Belgium are a hallucination due to group-hypnotism forms some measure of the value we need attribute to the same argument when it is applied to the New Testament. The conflict is more bitter. It is between light and darkness,

God and His enemies, Christ and Satan.
" For we wrestle not against flesh and blood,
but against principalities and powers, against
the rulers of the darkness of this world,
against spiritual wickedness in high places."

In conclusion, I must say that neither
here nor elsewhere is the Community of
the Resurrection to be held responsible for
anything that I have written. To my
brother, the Rev. Waldegrave Hart, C.R.,
my deep thanks are due. His time and
trouble have been given without stint in
the correction of the proofs.

I have also to thank, for permission to
make somewhat lengthy quotations, Messrs.
Macmillan & Co., Messrs. Williams &
Norgate, Messrs. Duckworth & Co., Messrs.
Burns & Oates, Messrs. T. & T. Clark,
Mr. T. N. Foulis, the Editor of *The
Hibbert Journal*, and Messrs. Longmans,
Green & Co.

J. NEVILLE FIGGIS.

House of the Resurrection,
        Mirfield,
            October 3, 1914.

CONTENTS

THE FELLOWSHIP OF THE
MYSTERY

THE FELLOWSHIP OF THE MYSTERY

I

"The fellowship of the mystery." (Ephes. iii. 9.)

"The Fellowship of the Mystery"; that is St. Paul's account of Churchmanship. It is a fellowship, a common life; and what is shared is a mystery, something that was once obscure, but is now in process of being made known. And this process goes on. However deep we go, there are yet farther deeps calling to us. No knowledge of God in Christ but opens the gate to a thousand fresh inquiries. The Christian Church, as throughout her history she catches echoes of the angels' song, is fitly symbolised by that loved one, now coming to the Kingdom, who was to be taught this:

3

" And I myself will teach to him,
   I myself, lying so ;
The songs I sing here ; which his voice
   Shall pause in, hushed and slow,
And find some knowledge at each pause,
   Or some new thing to know." [1]

" Some new thing to know ";—that is
the lot of man, whether of the Church or
of the world.　Even that portion of it which
once was " darkness," but is " now light in
the Lord," is still subject to this law.　Its
apprehension is never adequate to the
reality, least of all in religion.　It must
ever seek to adjust what of long time
has been its treasure with new forms of
thought and expression.　The more conservative minds may regret this tendency,
but they cannot escape it.　Even where
language remains unchanged, the whole
mental atmosphere has subtly altered; every
phrase becomes charged with fresh meaning,
symbolic perhaps of relations undreamed of
when it was first used.　Nor, on the other
hand, can the most revolutionary thinker
free himself from some dependence on the
past.　Vital in thought and imagination,
it has made the language in which he
reaches out to fresh adventures, so that he

---

[1] D. G. Rossetti, *The Blessed Damozel.*

cannot grasp the new except by instruments
that were forged upon ancient anvils.

In one regard it seems folly to set forth
our faith afresh, if we hold to historic creeds
and believe ourselves the guardians of a
"faith once delivered." Yet such effort is
not to be avoided, unless at the cost of the
entire deadness of what to us is the most
living of all things. Were it not possible
to bring faith into relation to the world,
as it lives now within us, it must sink (on
its intellectual side) into the utterance of
empty formulæ, which once were flames of
the spirit and have since become dried into
words, and—with such conditions—would
ere long be no more than sounds. "She
changes that she may remain the same"
were Newman's words of the Church ; and,
the moment we think of her as a living
spirit, not as a system or a code, we shall
see that this, which is a law of all our life
as persons, must hold good of this "holy
fellowship," and is indeed more vital in a
social union than in any individual.

Our age — the twentieth century — is
beyond others self-conscious. Like many
young minds, it is acutely aware of its own

novelty, and its difference from other times, especially that just passed. Its efforts to restate its faith in Christ are sometimes unduly emphatic. Often they resemble flights of that boyish exuberance which preens itself on a daring originality when it learns to realise that 2 and 2 make 4. But we pardon the simple conceits of youth, and rejoice that old truth has become vital to it, knowing that it is experience which makes commonplaces shine like stars. So, too, we may well be patient with the efforts of men in our day to make their faith in Christ vital once more, pathetic and often ludicrous as those attempts appear. So far as it is a living faith which they relate, even though the terms be crude and a little inadequate, we shall do well to take the will for the deed and see the striving Christian rather than the incomplete theologian. Sometimes, indeed, it is no faith in Christ at all, but merely a sentimental mysticism decorated with Christian phrases and decked in the shows of a piety which is in reality alien. That, however, is often not the case. What we shall do well to remember—I speak as a

Churchman to Churchmen—is this: we cannot ourselves escape the need of re-statement, and we are always making it, whether consciously or not. To doubt of this is to doubt the presence of the Holy Spirit in the Church. While we must hold that God has given to every age of the Christian Church all things needful to its salvation, it is not faith, but the denial of faith, to suppose that all was fixed finally and for ever by the close of the fourth General Council or by the sixth century, or by the thirteenth, or by the sixteenth, or by any other. If we can commit blas-phemy against the Holy Ghost, surely we shall be doing something very like it if we deny that He is speaking through God's Church in the twentieth century. Only let us bear in mind also that He spoke in the first, and will speak in the twenty-first. Heirs of all the ages, let us be slaves of none—not even our own. At least, how-ever, let us try to meet the good elements in the spirit of the twentieth century, eager as a child, avid of experience, hopeful, curious, adventurous—and, at the bottom of its heart, crying out for salvation (as witness the musings of Mr. Wells' hero in *Marriage*, as he lies ill in Labrador). Let us take away from our mode of presentment all that makes it harder than need be for the men of our day to discern the truth that the answer to all their restless longings is in one place only, Jesus Christ, and Him crucified.

In trying to think of a fitting topic for the Paddock Lectures, I was struck by the fact that they are to be delivered to a body consisting of ordained priests in God's Church and of those preparing for that holy function. Reflecting on this, and also on my own lack of an expert's acquaintance with those regions of critical inquiry which some now deem the sole meaning of theological study, it seemed to me that the contribution least likely to be useless might be some sort of consideration, not indeed of the grounds of theological truth or of the meaning of religion, but of the presentment of Churchmanship to the twentieth century by those who are unfeignedly loyal thereto. In the present lecture I should wish to think a little of its essential character as a gift of God; and in the second,

of the great Christian Society through
which this gift is made ours, and dwelling in which we are indeed at home, in
the centre of the spiritual experience of
the race. Then I should wish to go on
to show how the Church has not merely
a noble tradition to enshrine, but is the
hope of the future and has within her
the very spirit of all adventure. Fourthly,
we shall consider how that cry for self-
development and personality, now so loud
on all hands, receives its fulfilment in the
Gospel; and how even the asceticism of
the Church ever has this end in view, and
is, moreover, the natural and inevitable
method of all human progress, whether
individual or social. Fifthly, we shall say
something of the universality of a historic
and sacramental religion, and of its freedom
from that atmosphere, as of a spiritual
aristocracy, which attends all the more
individualistic forms of religion. Finally,
we shall be brought to consider the problem of authority and to discern its natural
and inevitable place in any social union,
and its part in the building of the Church;
and also to say a little of its limits and of

certain false notions as to its nature. These topics will be sufficient to occupy our six evenings; and if any here feel that they have the charm neither of erudition nor of novelty, I would crave to explain that neither erudition nor novelty are the things most needed at this moment by those who set forth Christ to men, but a hold on the inner realities of faith, and some conception of how to commend it to an age severely critical, but in some ways more ready to learn than the last two generations—if only we can persuade it to believe, first, that Christianity is the most interesting of all human phenomena, and secondly, that it is no mere wonder, but still that life which is the "light of men." Each of us needs to be able to feel of his message:

"I am a torch, and the flame of it is God,"[1]

and it is to make this a little more vivid that I am here to speak.

We are stewards of that "mystery"; so much we know and feel. What is this rare fellowship which unites us with

[1] Lascelles Abercrombie, *The Sale of Saint Thomas.*

men long gone, and separates us from some
now alive? What is this strange "It" of
which we have hold? For we have hold
of something, of that we are persuaded.
More deeply perhaps do we feel its reality
and uniqueness than any of the theories
as to what it is. So that first emerges as
our task in the face of modern men and
women. We stand for the distinctness
of the Christian experience—the unique,
incommunicable quality of the Christian
spirit, and for no mere general notion of religion. The Christian Church is something
more than a name for the spiritual aspects
of humanity; although here alone we reach
their final expression, and all other spiritual
systems point in some way to Christianity.
Unless we have something of our own as
Christians, and something which no other
religion has, it is idle to talk of missions;
idler still to hope to convert that sceptical,
critical, educated world which would come
to us if it were really convinced that ours
is the "pearl of great price," but would
have no need of our pictorial and historic
faith as a means of expressing a belief,
gained otherwise, that the universe makes

for good and that love is the highest law. In the last age things were different. In the heyday of materialistic advance, with the pre-suppositions of science largely unexamined, and the implications of a mechanical view of evolution in the air, men felt that the one thing needful to proclaim was the spiritual character of men and the universe and the unbending supremacy of the moral law; and that all who agreed to proclaim this were fighting for the same end against those who denied it. So they were. Now, however, that age is at an end. Materialism as a system has few votaries. The assumptions of science as a purely mechanical system are questioned on all hands. Religion is admittedly a factor in human life; and the problem is not whether or no we shall have a spirit of faith, but of what kind it shall be. For the seventies and eighties the question was, Can we save religion? It might be legitimate to assume that if this were answered in the affirmative the battle was won, and a ground secured in some way for Christianity, even though it should be necessary to clip its wings.

Now, however, we have begun to realise

that we are living in a new age, and that it will be an age of religion, or at least of religions. Men may oppose the Christian faith for many reasons:—because it is old, because it is in possession, because it is European, because it is socially unjust, because it persecuted in the past, because it seems dull, because it is Hebraic, because it is Hellenic, because it is Western, because it is Eastern, because it teaches self-denial, because it preaches a heaven of bliss, because it appeals to high motives, because it fosters low ideals,—on any and every contradictory ground men will condemn our Church; but less and less will they condemn her simply and solely on the ground that she is a religion. It is religion they are crying for, struggling for, determined in some way or other to get; although I grant that they do not for the most part expect to find what they are seeking in the Christian Church. It is we who have to convince them that their error lies not in seeking, but in seeking to slake their thirst for God anywhere but in Christ. The world to-day is very much like the soul in Francis Thompson's greatest poem, which

went through all experiences in a vain
search for joy, only to find it at last in Him :

> " Halts by me that footfall:
> Is my gloom, after all,
> Shade of His hand, outstretched caressingly ?
> Ah, fondest, blindest, weakest,
> I am He Whom thou seekest !
> Thou dravest love from thee, who dravest Me." [1]

Besides, science has awakened to religion
as a human fact. Religion as an integral
element in human life is taken for granted.
Religious phenomena are studied, classified
and analysed; and a mass of formulated
knowledge now exists which serves at least
to throw light on their origin and early
development, beyond anything that would
have been held likely fifty years ago. Religion is admitted to be a normal, if not
a universal human activity; and the attitude
of the militant materialist of the past has
now few respectable exponents. Doubtless
in this, as in all ages, there are sheer ration-
alists, just as there are practical material-
ists or active pagans; and there are further
definite survivals of past forms of thought
and feeling. Still, I think it is not unfair

---

[1] Francis Thompson, *The Hound of Heaven.*

to say that at this moment the question most of us have to decide is not whether or no religion is proper to human life, but what kind of religion it is to be.   On that ground, if on no other, and through the very presence of the adversary, Christianity will be forced to realise its own distinctness like a flame. Mr. Benjamin Kidd, who in his famous work, *Social Evolution*, argued so strongly in favour of a religious view of the world as opposed to one purely intellectualistic or rationalist in the narrow sense, set forth in a second book, *Principles of Western Civilisation*, the very strongest ground for supposing that Christianity could maintain itself, in so far as it does maintain itself, only in face of an all-round fire of criticism more acute than any previously known ; and that effort, apart from all other considerations, will automatically bring about, on the part of all who cling to the Christian hope, a greater sense of its uniqueness and an intenser bond of union.

But this is not all.   This acceptance of religion is not likely to make our task easier to-day, and in some ways is apt to lead to a bitter hostility to all attempts to make of the Christian faith anything distinctive or real. The great thing is felt to be personal religious experience; and historical Christianity is by no means the only form in which this has been found. It is, moreover, bound up with certain modes of thought and traditions of a past culture which are now only entanglements, and cannot be entirely separated. Why should we sing the songs David sang—or did not sing, for the matter of that? And why should the twentieth-century woman go to St. Paul to school? Mystical knowledge too, the only direct and immediate form of religious knowledge, although not absent from the Christian Church, has by no means its exclusive home therein. Local and provincial elements appear in much of the history and cult of the Christian Church; and we are too wise to suspect that a religion which is the crystallisation of Western history is the last word of spiritual progress. All this has tended to a contemptuous tolerance which does lip-service to the Founder of Christianity, but has no faith in any of the institutions which have come out of His life, and treats the

Church as merely one among many developments of the religious spirit; and, even when it admits that it has so far been the noblest and most pure, regards it as a transient episode now at an end, and sees in the unrest of the age the birth pangs of some new synthesis which will supersede this cult of a crucified Hebrew with its Babylonian cosmogony and magical accretions. More hostile of course are many, both to Christian doctrine and to ethics; but we need not at length consider them. What I want to bring out here is the fact that if we are to stand for anything just now, it must be for some distinct incommunicable glory in the Christian religion—its own crown and not another's—and that we must be prepared to have to fight.

The fact that it has this quality will not be doubted by any of us, so far as his own religion is a real thing. It is the inspiration of all mission work, the motive of every Eucharist, the meaning of every conversion, the unconscious presupposition of every Christian assembly; although (be it observed) it is not, and never will be, the assumption of those persons to whom religion is mainly a social convention, or of those thinkers to whom it is but a convenient symbol, historical in the West, for the ideal aspirations of humanity.

This sense that we as Christians have a treasure lacking to others need lead us to no Pharisaical denial of great goodness and self-devotion among the votaries of other faiths, and even among agnostics; although we shall do well to be on our guard against the tendency to judge other systems by their rarest products, and our own by the "average sensual man." John Stuart Mill is no type of the normal product of any system. Nor need we suppose that the knowledge of God in all other faiths is negligible or perverse;[1] indeed, we could not approach them if we did; free to honour what is noble in other faiths, we have much to learn therefrom. But we are bound to set out our conviction that we have something of which they do not know; that in this treasure we have a joy they cannot fathom; and that, on the whole, and allow-

[1] See on this point some valuable remarks in Mr. T. J. Hardy's new book, *The Religious Instinct*, chapter iii., "The Interpretation of Instinct; § 2. The Interpretive nature of Christianity obscured by the monopolist school."

ing for the necessary limitations, our community of the Church has tended to produce
human life at its highest general level and
to endow it with the richest activities. That
treasure we believe to be the Gift of God—
eternal life in Christ Jesus our Lord. The
supreme difference of the Christian religion
is this fact, that it is the gift of a new life—
not a code, or a creed, or an achievement,
but a spirit given.

Half the errors which beset us now come
from the common refusal to recognise this
truth. Calvinism as a system was hideous,
and is in no way to be reconciled with the
doctrine that God is Love—about which
doctrine, in truth, Calvin never troubled
himself, being content to elaborate a purely
deductive theory of damnation derived from
the notion of monarchical sovereignty, as
conceived according to absolutist legalism.
Yet even Calvinism had this merit, lacking
in the facile optimism of modern sentiment-
ality, that it laid stress on the two cardinal
truths of (1) the need of man, (2) the given-
ness of God's grace.

It is in this sense of the gift of life to
a creature dying, from a Power which is

beyond the world, that lies hidden all the distinct and peculiar aroma of the Christian life. The transcendence of God as complementary to His immanence, His love and Fatherhood, the very core of His nature, the fact of revelation, the grace of redemption, the all-penetrating gift of life, and the union between this world and that beyond—all these conceptions, or values, I do not say are logically deducible from the idea of the gift, but they are bound together so closely with it, that if we lose hold of the one, we shall find it hard to retain the other.

All this we who are to be Christian priests need at this moment to emphasise, or else we may come to be deluded by the catchwords of that very trend towards religion of which we spoke. Unquestionably, the interest in religious experience is all around us; and it has dangers of its own. Men begin hunting for the thrills of a high ecstasy. They turn too exclusively to its psychological side, tending to treat religion as the expression of certain moods or temperaments, and forget the Supreme Object of it all. As Father Kelly has said in his recent valuable work on *The Church and Religious Unity :*

" With intentions the most passionately
" sincere, nay, just because of its sincerity,
" Protestantism failed to see the confusions
" in which it was involving itself—the con-
" fusion between *faith in God* Who is more
" than man, and *faith in faith*, that is, in
" a feeling of assurance, which is a virtue
" and a feeling of man." [1]

We are reaping nowadays the results of this error, in the excessive subjectivism of much modern religion, and the denial of all need of any outside reality. It is this great fact, that the Christian (if his witness be true) has been granted a " grace," a "somewhat living" that "came down from Heaven," which gives him his peculiar stamp. This ought to be the enduring foundation of our work. This meets, as nothing else can, the needs of the spirit, and by its inherent power will once more win for the Christian Church new triumphs; while she may change in many ways and lose some merely local and temporary colour-ings which have sometimes been her weak-

[1] pp. 90, 91.

ness, sometimes her strength, and are now
by many regarded as evidence of her near
decay. For this gift taken in its fulness
—eternal life in Christ Jesus our Lord—
ministers to three permanent, irreducible
needs of the soul: the need for intimacy
between man's spirit and the eternal, which
is met by the life in Christ; the need for
a voice from the world beyond, assuring
him of a life beyond life, and the conser-
vation of value, in which one religious
philosopher (Höffding) places the meaning
of religion; and the need for deliverance,
for some hope of redemption of a world
which cries loudly for salvation and can be
satisfied with nothing less than a Redeemer.
True, indeed, these needs are not felt by
everyone; perhaps no one is equally conscious of all three; and some would deny
them all. Yet I think that with the
admission that religious experience is a
thing normal to human life, we may take
it as given that these three wants are a
natural element in the make-up of man—intimacy, otherworldliness, redemption; these
are of the essence of the gift, and of the
essence of the need; without any one of

them no religion can give us what we ask.

All this is no proof that the Christian faith is justified in its claim to satisfy them. Some will deem their very existence a ground for rejecting it—on the plea that the whole Christian scheme owes its origin to their presence, and that the doctrine of redemption, through faith in the Incarnate and Risen Lord, is but the expression of our subjective needs creating a dream world wherein to rest. All arguments for the congruity of our essential creed with the facts of human life may be turned into grounds for denying its objective basis; for the more we can discern the relation between the Christian ideal and the strivings of the human soul, the more possible must we admit it to be— especially in an age which knows a little about the development of Christian theology —that the whole was due to the imagination, to the sense that what men so very much wanted must somehow be the fact.

Many of the most devout souls are at this hour torn by the fear lest it all be due

to self-hypnotism. Even at the moment
of some sacrifice for Christ's sake they
are faced with the doubt—what if there
be no Christ? To such hesitations there
can be no final reply. We cannot demonstrate these matters any more than you
can demonstrate to the solipsist the fact
that there is a world beyond himself. The
problems of a historical religion, entangled
in the concrete and the inevitable uncer-
tainties of evidence, must be accepted as
an initial difficulty; you cannot have a
historical religion without them. That,
however, is no ground for taking the course,
recommended in some quarters, of giving
up all reliance on the historical side of
Christianity on account of the difficulties
inherent in the evidence. No course would
seem less wise or more destructive of the
very nature of that religion we seek to
defend.

As Westcott well knew:

" A religion which is to move the world
"must be based on a history. A religion
"drawn solely from the individual con-
"sciousness of man can only reflect a par-
"ticular form of intellectual development.

"Its influence is limited by the mould in
"which it is cast. Its applicability is con-
"fined to those who have attained to a
"special culture. Even to the last it is
"essentially of the mind and not of the
"heart or of the life. This is obvious
"equally from the speculations of Natural
"Theology, and from the history of all
"those religions which have had any power
"in the world. A subjective religion brings
"with it no element of progress and cannot
"lift man out of himself. A historical
"revelation alone can present God as an
"object of personal love. The external
"world answering to human instinct sug-
"gests the conception of His eternal power,
"but offers nothing which justifies us in
"the confidence of 'sons.' Man is but one
"of the many elements of creation and
"cannot arrogate to himself any special
"relationship with his Maker. Pure Theism
"is unable to form a living religion.
"Mohammedanism lost all religious power
"in a few generations. Judaism survived
"for fifteen centuries every form of assault
"in virtue of the records of a past de-
"liverance on which it was based, and the

" hope of a future Deliverer which it in-
" cluded." [1]

Nor is this even the counsel of prudence.
We need indeed to rid ourselves of the
contemporary bias not so much against
miracle as against the existence, in any
active way, of a spirit world beyond our
own.

But this is a digression. I do not to-
day desire to spend your time in labouring
this point, partly because many have done
so in this place who are far better equipped
than I, partly because I am speaking to
those who are themselves Christians, partly
because I have elsewhere spoken of it a
little. Two things, however, may perhaps be said without impertinence. When
people talk, as they will do, of the decay of
Christian belief, and picture the parlous state
of the educated world, we need not dismiss
their fears as of no moment and make
ourselves at home in a fool's paradise.
Too often this has been done at the price
of disaster; an ostrich-like policy is the
danger even now of many priests. But we
are free to reflect on the facts of history.

---

[1] *The Gospel of the Resurrection* (Macmillan), pp. 8, 9.

Above all, the lesson of the eighteenth century and the subsequent revival should
cheer us in hours of gloom. Secondly, in
regard to the detailed criticism of the New
Testament, we are not to forget—as many
would have us—that we have to do with the
origin of the mightiest phenomenon known
in history, and that the probabilities of its
origin being a little uncommon are not in-
considerable. Further, let us read the New
Testament through, and judge whether we
have not here a single, deep, and massive
impression, that of the action of forces
best qualified as supernatural; whether we
do not gain that view alike from the letters
of St. Paul, from the accounts of the
growth of the Church in the Acts, from
the portrait of the Lord Jesus in the
Synoptic Gospels, and from His inner
mind revealed to us in the Fourth Gospel
and the first Epistle of St. John. That
impression we may think false; but can we
do that without throwing over the whole
New Testament, and without leaving the
phenomenon of Christianity, which has been
growing ever since and *still is growing*, with
an explanation, which, however superficially

plausible, is not even historically satisfactory? Do we, in fact, know enough either about man or the world to reject what is the most obvious and natural view of this pheno-menon? And if we reject it, let us con-sider whither such rejection will logically lead us; and ask ourselves whether we are prepared, on a reflection of all the facts of our own inner life and of the world around us, to reach that logical goal. If we have the courage of our doubts, perhaps we shall find, by contemplating this ex-treme issue, that they lead to a *reductio ad absurdum*.

As one honoured in this place writes:

" Most men do not follow their doubts far
" enough to discover whither they ultimately
" lead. The advice sometimes given, 'Crush
" your doubt, drive it out by an act of will,'
" is not only practically ineffective, but of
" dubious ethical value as well. The doubt
" so crushed returns to haunt one as the
" ghost of a possible truth. . . . This follow-
" ing up of doubts to the bitter end has a
" tonic effect on the spirit. When doubt
" suggests difficulties as to the Christian re-
" velation, let it rob the world of the Gospel

"of the Incarnate God. But do not let it
"stop there, press it hard until it has piled
"up its objections to the doctrine of a
"Loving Father; and the earth is left for-
"lorn and orphaned, wheeling through space
"—the victim of nought but inexorable
"law. But doubts may not logically stop
"even here; let them play havoc with all
"the most cherished ideals of the heart.
"With God the sense of moral obligation
"must go, at least as soon as the voice of
"conscience is clearly understood to be
"only nature's blind sanction of methods
"which conserve the propagation of the
"race. Let your doubt sweep unopposed
"through the whole gamut of possible
"scepticisms until love and beauty and
"righteousness are explained away. There
"are patent objections to the spiritual in-
"terpretation of them all. And then, when
"you have at last arrived at the goal and
"look about in the drear desert,—without
"meaning, without motive, without hope—
"ask yourself whether you can, or care to,
"live in the land of doubt." [1]

Here, however, what we have to do is to

[1] Robbins, *An Essay Toward Faith*, pp. 42–46. (Longmans, Green & Co.)

insist on the fact that the "fellowship of
the mystery" means the sharing in a gift
which we believe to have come in a definite
historical Person, of which we believe
ourselves to have adequate evidence in the
Church in the written documents, and
against which, the more that is known
about the constitution of matter, of nature,
and of life, the less plausible seem the
objections. So we may go on to consider a
little more of the nature of the gift. First
and foremost, it is the gift to man's memory
and imagination of a definite, concrete,
historical individual, Jesus of Nazareth.
Let us never forget this or lose sight of it.
Persons living largely among books, and
concerned mainly with schemes and notions,
may deem it an easy thing to treat this as
of no moment. Such men may like to
think that the concrete historical facts
having sufficed to start off the system of
ideas—the Fatherhood of God and the
brotherhood of man, and so forth—it is of
small matter whether or no there be any
actual historical basis for the picture of the
poor Man of Galilee, Who blessed the
children and won the sinners and healed

sick people and irritated the respectable religious and denounced the rich. Believe me, it is not so. Only for a very small number (even in an age when education was widely diffused) would this realm of ideas even apparently be enough. The charm of Christianity lies in its excessive concreteness; not merely is God seen embodied in man, but He comes to us, not as one of the more abstract and speculative classes aloof from the crowd, but Emmanuel, God with us. It is to the crib and the baby that men look, to the boy in the temple, to the strange preacher of goodness, the friend of Lazarus, to the sufferer of Gethsemane, the confronter of Pilate and Herod, and, above all, to the "strange Man on the Cross." This it is which pulls the heart out of humanity, and gives to Jesus an undying attraction for men who sin and women who suffer and boys and girls who love and quarrel. It is vain to hurl against us the obvious fact, as though it were a new discovery, that Jesus was not a philosopher or an author or an art critic. Who ever said He was ? The whole point of His life lies in the fact that He was not.   As Mandell Creighton put it:

"He mixed Himself in no parties of "religion or politics. He laboured not to "form a sect or to set forth a system of "practice or belief, which should satisfy the "logical requirements of subtle minds. "There fell from His lips, as occasion drew "them forth, fragments of a wisdom which "men felt to be Divine. There was shed "from His life, as He moved in lowliness, "gleams of a glory which this world could "not give. By the loftiness of a soul that "was free from this world and the things "of this world, He still draws the hearts of "all men unto Him.

"As we gaze on Him, we must feel the "littleness of our best intentions, of our "highest efforts. He came forward as the "champion of no system. He advocated "no plans of social reform. He did none "of those things on which we pride our- "selves as our noblest and best undertak- "ings. He only lived amongst men and "loved them; and the effects of that life "and of that love will last for ever." [1]

[1] *University Sermons*, p. 89.

Modern criticism, with all its faults, has at heart the right instinct for the realisation of the Man Christ Jesus, the sense that here is the centre of the interest of mankind. Without Jesus, Christianity might be a very noble creation, and could theoretically contain the ethic of love; but in practice it would be something quite different, as indeed it always is for those (whether orthodox or not) for whom Christianity is mainly a body of speculative doctrines instead of loyalty to a living Person. Their religion is always lacking in charm; and, even where technically correct, it has no winning or missionary power. The modern Lutheran, Hermann, is right in insisting that first and foremost must come the impression of this, the astounding concrete reality, "The Man Christ Jesus."[1] Hard though it be to define personality and to discover the exact nature of its limits in a speculative way, it yet remains true that for the ordinary man or woman (as he will be under any phase of culture) it is not hard to conceive of the highest ideal as embodied in a concrete historic life, and

[1] *Cf.* Hermann, *The Communion of the Christian with God.*

that any other would always leave out some essential part. If Jesus had spoken only as a thinker, or even as a moral teacher, He could have given men no more than a system of reforms or a code of precepts; instead, He has given us Himself, "the same yesterday, to-day, and for ever."

But this is not all. The gift is not merely that of the impression of a historical personality; it is the power of a loving intimacy. The revelation of a perfect life would indeed have much to strengthen and to elevate mankind; we are all of us the better for the great ones who have gone before. But mere loyalty to a memory is not the whole of our religion; and, however inspiring, a religion so limited would lack many elements. The gift we have is that of a real personal intimacy with One Who is not merely man but God, and the assurance of a union beyond life with Him Who overcame Death. For the human soul is so made that, while conscious of the greatness of the forces which environ it, and also of its own distinctness, it yet craves for an intimacy, a communion more

intense than any earthly friendship and
without its flaws; nor may it at the last
be satisfied, unless it can be one with the
Eternal. Man is a wanderer upon earth;
but he seeks a home at the heart of things.
That home is assured him, while his own
individual being is still preserved, by the
Christian doctrine of Eternal Life; the
belief that God is so powerful that He can
limit His own power in the Incarnation,
and so humbly loving that He did so. The
supreme and most difficult act of Divine
omnipotence is His Self-limitation; and
it is conditioned only by humility in God,
which is the true expression of His nature
as Love; and even now it shows so stupen-
dous that those who long for it can barely
credit their ears, and many find it too hard
for them.

Religion is fundamentally concerned with
the other world. Ultimately, the criterion of any religion lies in what it has
to tell us of Death. In the Resurrection
of our Lord and His Ascended Glory we
have the most amazing of all the riches of
that gift to man which we call the Gospel.
Here again, despite the clamour of a faith-

less criticism, there is nothing really to shake our belief in its historical reality. To quote once more from Dean Robbins:

" Criticism . . . has not yet even suggested " a plausible explanation on merely natural " grounds of the great crucial fact of the " Resurrection of Jesus Christ from the " dead." [1]

What was the mode of His rising may be a problem; but the Resurrection, as an actual vital objective fact, stands as the historical basis of the Church. It fills the first place in the early preaching of St. Paul, and makes the gist of the apologetic of St. Peter. Nor can there be any ground for our surrendering this belief merely to gratify a body of critics who start with a presupposition against it. The only basis on which it can really be doomed is the unstated postulate, either that the other world has no reality or that it has no point of contact with this. Eager though we may be for new light, let us beware of being false to the vision which nerved the saints and martyrs, or of surrendering lightly, as in panic, beliefs which have made

[1] Robbins, *An Essay Towards Faith*, p. 32.

it true that if the Gospel be not a Gospel of the Resurrection, it would for most people cease to be a Gospel at all.

The gift of God is not merely in Jesus, as the brightness of His Being, nor even in our communion with the Risen Life. It lies in the great Act upon the Cross, where by His one sacrifice once offered He "made a full, perfect, and sufficient sacrifice, oblation, and satisfaction for the sins of the whole world." Mankind, as a whole, needs not so much revelation as redemption. It is not a theoretical problem, but a practical trouble, that drives men to Christ. Most that I have said so far might be true even if there were no sin. If all things had grown together in harmony and there were no sense of a world awry, man, being what he is, would still have need of a character in which perfect Love was embodied, of that hope of a life beyond of which the Resurrection assures him. But how different in fact is our state! How impossible to-day are the optimistic dreams of speculative enthusiasts, the comfortable theories about the "best of all possible worlds" and the "pre-established harmony"! Grim as

may be that picture of the universe which
Nietzsche makes us feel like a drama, with
its blind "will to power" driving men to
impotence, and its tale of suffering and evil,
of cruelty and pride, told once and retold
for ever; dark as may be the pessimism of
Hartmann, to whom consciousness is an
evil, and whose only hope is a self-annihilation of all things—even these doctrines
and their counterpart in the East testify to
facts.   They are nearer to reality than the
rose-water sentimentalism which sees progress inevitable in every revolution of the
earth on its axis, and mocks the tears of
humanity with the blasphemy that evil is
only evil on a partial view, and that from
the standpoint of the whole there is nought
but good.

All such views, whether embodied in the
ancient religions of the East or in the philo-
sophies of nineteenth-century students, have
faced the central tragedy of things; and, if
wrong about the cause, they are right about
the fact.   As it stands, the world needs redemption.   No faith which does not offer
salvation can hope for the allegiance of the
great mass of men.   This—the need of

deliverance—is the burden of all our socio-
logical writers; it is the cat's-paw even
of politicians, who may not see far but
must have some real leverage; and it is
once more beginning to be felt to be the
supreme glory of Christianity, that it meets
the need. What gives it its power, its
élan vital through the course of history, is
this fact of its being a redemption, a new
life. We can see it vibrating through the
Epistles of St. Paul, calm and self-resting
in St. John, and triumphant in St. Peter
and the Apocalypse. By those who look
at it as thinkers or as students, too much
attention is often paid to the thought of
Christianity as a Revelation. That indeed it is; but it is only that on account
of its great practical end, the salvation of
man. Its aim is not to satisfy his curious
interest, but to make that possible which
otherwise were not possible, to restore a
union which by man's own act and deed
is broken, to win a pardon, which, even
when he repudiates it, his inmost being
craves. I am persuaded that we who are
guardians of the gift are worse than foolish
if we preach the Christian faith mainly

as the Incarnation or the Resurrection, and put into the second place the thought of Jesus Christ and Him Crucified. The doctrine of the Atonement is not fully clear to us; but is there any doctrine which is? Much thinking needs to be done thereon, and perhaps this age may contribute something.[1] But it is this fact of forgiveness which turns the creed into the Gospel and converts the sinner. No other religious system offers an adequate substitute for this, although doubtless the sacrificial system of the ancients may have led the way thereto. Where sacrifice is practised to-day it is a symbol of the same need. The Cross of Christ is the supreme gift of God to man, the act which gave life to the dead; and on that ground it is the revelation of the love which is the heart of reality, and the assurance that no true sacrifice is vain.

As a Nonconformist divine who has done much to set this doctrine in the light declares:

---

[1] *e.g.* Professor Royce's theory that a true sacrifice increases values to a greater extent than selfishness had diminished them.

" Every ray of intellectual light we have
" is to force, and enable us the better to
" put, the question, ' Where am I ? ' ' What
" doest thou here, Elijah ? ' It is not a
" question, ' What do I hold ? ' but, ' How
" do I behave to what holds me ? ' It is
" not, ' What can I make of the world ? ' but,
" ' How do I stand to what is given me in
" the world ? ' It is not, ' What do I know ? '
" but, ' How far do I realise that I am
" known ? ' It is not, ' How do I conceive
" the divine truth of the world ? ' but, ' How
" do I meet the divine action in the world ? '
" Not, ' Do I see the cohesion of God's great
" truth ? ' but, ' Do I gauge and answer the
" bearing of God's eternal act ? ' Not, ' How
" do I feel about God ? ' but, ' What deal-
" ings have I with Him ? ' Our first con-
" cern is not with the riddle of the Universe;
" it is with the tragedy of the Universe." [1]

[1] Rev. P. T. Forsyth in *The Hibbert Journal*, January 1913, pp. 318, 319.

II

THE INSEPARABLE SOCIETY

"The lines are fallen unto me in pleasant places; yea,
"I have a goodly heritage." (Psalm xvi. 6.)

In our first lecture we were trying to see a
little of what is meant by saying that other
foundation can no man lay save Christ Jesus.
To-day I wish to speak of the means by
which we approach Christ, namely that social
unity which is the living earthly expression
of His being, and of the necessity of this
means.   Not all admit that necessity.

Ever since the beginning of modern individualism, and indeed earlier, an unmediated union with Christ has been the
dream of many; just as an unmediated union
with God is the cry of some who reject
the mediatorial office of our Saviour.
Churchmen are for ever being met with
the taunt that they have placed another
between God and the soul.   Further, a
belief in a direct vision of God, apart from

all outward means, is the thesis of that mysticism now so much in fashion. No one, perhaps, need be concerned to deny that this direct communion of our souls with God is the enduring substratum of all religion, and that public worship, sacramental life, and ecclesiastical institutions of all kinds are successful, or the reverse, according as they reach, or fail to reach, that end. For all that, if this union is to have any claim to be a knowledge of Christ Jesus, the need of mediation comes in at once. Not only can a merely personal experience of God's power have no guarantee against its being self-deception, but, apart from the Church and all which that implies, it can afford us no means of learning that what we come in contact with is Jesus of Nazareth. Our Lord may speak to the soul alone, it is true; but we cannot proceed to identify His voice with that of Jesus Christ without the use of historical knowledge, and that will be found to imply the Church.

Whatever our religion is to mean to us after we have it, we cannot gain even a minimum acquaintance with Jesus except through the institutions that issued from

His life, or their products such as the New
Testament.   Even the most extreme Protestant must perforce make use of the
Church before he can reach to any idea of
our Lord.   Since He no longer walks the
earth, all knowledge of His historical life can
come to us only through institutions which
express His spirit, or through documents
and relics.   So far as any of these institutions do embody His spirit, they give us
a living knowledge of Him.   Yet even
the documents and other historical *débris*
which serve as evidence are of the nature
of mediation.   They tell us what others
have thought and said about Him, and
what He Himself did and said; they are,
however, not Jesus Christ, but a means to
knowledge of Him.   Nor is this all.   Even
these documents have an origin which is
social.   More and more are we coming to
see that any literature which is alive is to
be grasped only if we view it as a social
product.   In like manner the New Testament is the outgrowth of the Church and
its first expression.   Man is incurably
social; and he can obtain no contact with
any world-historical figure which is not

mediated by the social order which helped to express him. We approach Julius Cæsar by going back from institutions still alive, the title Kaiser, the Roman law, places, names, &c. &c., to all the sources of our knowledge of those things; and in like manner we are driven, however reluctantly, to approach our Lord Jesus Christ through those social institutions of which His life was the originating principle.

Fallacious and unreal is the notion that we can study Jesus Christ in the abstract, and then, if we so please, pass on to a private intercourse with Him. It comes from an unreal conception of the nature of historical knowledge, conditioned by the abstraction of study. History does not exist spread out in all its beauty before us, like New York City, so that you can begin where the taxi-cab stops, go in any direction you please, and ignore the rest. There is only one real date in history—now.

What is the meaning of all historical, no less than of all scientific, inquiry? An explanation, or at least an account, of something that strikes us here and now. We might say that we study history in order

to understand the newspapers. At any
moment any individual is confronted with
a large complex of social facts, peoples,
nations, languages, states, churches, clubs,
families, trades, games, topics of argument, clothes, objects of art; and if he
asks of any of these how it came to be, he
is driven to a long regress, and ultimately
to an account of world history. We must
get some notion of history before we can
realise ourselves. The conception of evolution, so far from making this more difficult,
makes it easier; for it links together historical and scientific studies. Science gives us
the history of the physical universe rather
than its explanation.

So with the case before us. The fact
that comes before men to-day is the
outward visible phenomena of buildings,
institutions, and persons, who in some way
or other hark back to Christ. In order to
have any adequate notion of what they all
mean, we are forced back and back through
the ages of Church history, towards the
New Testament, and eventually behind it.
We do not begin with the year one, as
though it were something self-existing;

we can get to it only by means of evidence of one kind or another. Not only to Christianity, but also to historical culture, harm is being done by this abstract, speculative way of looking at history, fixing an arbitrary date—1066, 1688, 1776, and so forth—instead of trying to show the student that history is merely the account of how things have come to be what they are, and that our one fixed datum is our own consciousness at the moment.

Secondly, the notion of a purely individualist religion is false to the nature of man. In politics the old contractual individualistic theories of civil society are gone; not one of us but can smile at the crudely individualist conceptions of the State entertained by Jeremy Bentham, and even Herbert Spencer. Nowadays we are all concerned with the mind of the crowd, group personality, social psychology, and so forth. How can we go on entertaining in regard to religion—which, as a fact, has been the most binding of all social unions—conceptions as to the relation of the individual to the society which have been shown to be inadequate for every other form of com-

munal life, from a golf club to an empire?
Churchliness in some form or other is bound
to be the religion of the future. A curious
evidence of this is to be found in the
presentment of Christianity offered by
Professor Royce in his work on *The Problem of Christianity*. The purely social communal side of Christianity is over-emphasised
in this book, and the relation of the individual soul to the historic Christ, Jesus
of Nazareth, is minimised; yet, in view
of the individualist character of developed
Protestantism, the pronouncement of the
Harvard philosopher in favour of authority,
social redemption, and loyalty to a body, is
no less wholesome than it is remarkable.
To many of us the formula " Christianity
is Christ " has seemed illuminating; but it
is dangerous if not explained. The thesis
of Professor Royce in this most interesting
book is precisely the opposite ; Christianity
is loyalty—loyalty to the " Beloved Community." I quote one or two passages :

" The value of loyalty can readily be de-
" fined in simply human terms. Man, the
" social being, naturally, and in one sense
" helplessly, depends on his communities.

" Sundered from them, he has neither worth
" nor wit, but wanders in waste places, and,
" when he returns, finds the lonely house
" of his individual life empty, swept, and
" garnished.

" But, on the other hand, his communities,
" to which he thus owes all his natural
" powers, train him by teaching him self-
" will, and so teach him the arts of spiritual
" hatred. The result is distraction, spiritual
" death. Escape through any mere multi-
" tude of loves for other individuals is im-
" possible. For such loves, unless they are
" united by some supreme loyalty, are
" capricious fondnesses for other individuals,
" who, by nature and by social training, are
" as lonely and as distracted as their lover
" himself. Mere altruism is no cure for
" the spiritual disease of cultivation. . . .

" Loyalty, if it comes at all, has the value
" of a love which does not so much re-
" nounce the individual self as devote the
" self, with all its consciousness and its
" powers, to an all-embracing unity of in-
" dividuals in one realm of spiritual har-
" mony. The object of such devotion is,
" in ideal, the community which is abso-

D

" lutely lovable, because absolutely united,
" conscious, but above all distractions of
" the separate self-will of its members.
" Loyalty demands many members, but one
" body; many gifts, but one spirit." [1]

It is right that this reminder should come
from the philosopher. For in truth churchliness is involved in personality. Long ago
Aristotle taught that the " State is prior to
the individual." True, neither the theory
nor the practice of the antique city-state
sufficiently allowed for the distinctness of
individuality; and it was the Christian
Church, as even Nietzsche admitted, that
first saw the worth of each man as an end,
not a means. Yet for all that, Aristotle's
maxim expresses one great truth—that the
individual cannot come to himself except in
a society. That is the ever-repeated lesson
of the family, the school, the college, and
of all the thousand and one developments
of the associative principle in life. Apart
from a society, a man could not be a human
being; he would have no language. Each
member brings his own contribution. But,
from the day of our birth to that of our

---

[1] See Royce, o.c., vol. i. p. 188. (Macmillan & Co.)

death, we have no means of acting as individuals, however eccentric, which are not mainly the creation of society, and of many different forms of society. When some plutocrat complains of old-age pensions or insurance as likely to injure the sturdy independence of the poor and destroy that individual energy which is the backbone of the nation, one is tempted to inquire how much the speaker knows of his own debt to social institutions. Does he not owe his Christian name to one society, his surname to another, his wealth to a long course of historical influences, his security to a law which is essentially the expression of social unity? It is indeed the height of absurdity to talk as though the freedom of the richer classes to be individualist were not the creation of a society in which they live.[1] So it is with religion. The most unattached Christian, provided his Christianity be a real union with "the Man Christ Jesus," could never have secured that union were it not for those institutions which have expressed

[1] The interest of Professor Royce's book lies largely in the penetrating analysis of the social consciousness, and the way in which it awakens the individual alike to loyalty and to rebellion.

His Personality on earth; nor could he use the language of devotion without the help of many generations of Christian life in society. Moreover, even when he rejects all this, such rejection implies a knowledge and conception of that social life, and is not in reality a private union independent of it. The Society of Friends, the most purely subjective form of Protestantism, would never have been possible had it not been for the atmosphere provided by the Church.

To quote Professor Royce again :

" It is our fellows who first startle us out "of our natural unconsciousness about our "own conduct; and who then, by an endless "series of processes of setting us attractive "but difficult models, and of socially interfer- "ing with our own doings, train us to higher "and higher grades and to more and more "complex types of self-consciousness regard- "ing what we do and why we do it. Play and "conflict, rivalry and emulation, conscious "imitation and conscious social contrasts "between man and man,—these are the "source of each man's consciousness about "his own conduct." [1]

[1] Royce, o.c., i. p. 132.

"All experience must be *at least* individual "experience; but unless it is *also* social "experience, and unless the whole religious "community which is in question unites to "share it, this experience is but as sounding "brass, and as a tinkling cymbal. This "truth is what Paul saw. This is the rock "upon which the true and ideal Church is "built. This is the essence of Christianity.

"If indeed I myself must cry 'out of the "depths' before the light can come to me, "it must be my Community that, in the "end, saves me. To assert this and to live "this doctrine constitute the very core of "Christian experience."[1]

Once more, the notion of individualist Christianity is foreign to the Gospel. That religion which teaches the fatherhood of God and the brotherhood of man, of which the cardinal maxim is to love God and one another, must inevitably be the most penetrating of all forms of social union. What Christianity does is to carry to their full conclusion the implications of human nature and the lessons of political union.[2] A faith

[1] Royce, Preface, vol. i. p. xvi.
[2] *Cf.* on this point, *Personality as a Philosophical Principle*, by the Rev. Wilfrid Richmond; also an extremely valuable and

which is the living expression of mutual love
cannot be satisfied by a society which sub-
sists on a basis of contract, with the individual free to leave it while still remaining
a full Christian. Love is the most penetrating of all forces. It unites the spirits of
men, not merely their minds. Where it is
real, it expresses itself in a mutuality of
intercourse which is deeper than can be put
into words, and changes the whole personality. We must not figure the membership of the Church like a heap of pebbles,
which are unchanged as they lie together;
rather is it a union of many diverse
elements, all constantly changing and acting
upon each other, such as we see in some
fair meadow, lit by sunshine after rain,
wherein all things—from the chemical in-
gredients of the grasses and the lines of the
flowers to the constituents of the stream
that flows through it, to the colours of the
sky and the cloud-shadows, and the songs

more recent work, *Personality*, by Dr. F. B. Jevons, especially the
last chapter on "Individuality," in which the author shows the
fallacy alike of Absolutistic Monism and of the view of imper-
meable individuality, which in the long run means Solipsism.
Further, on the interpenetration of spiritual beings, *cf.* Webb,
Problems in the Relation to God and Man.

of the birds and the humming of the little insects, and the quiver of the butterfly-wings—are each and all affected and, affecting each other, yet unite to create a whole which is a deeper harmony than any human work of art, because it is alive and changes in all its parts from moment to moment. Such is our relation to one another and to the Sun of Righteousness in the Christian Church.

The purely individualist notion of Christianity is shattered on the rock of man's social nature, and also on that foundation fact of our life, the Communion of Saints. Quakerism, for instance, in its doctrine of the Inner Light, is independent of all creeds, and is not fundamentally even Christian; for it has nothing but a subjective criterion. Moreover, in its rejection of every kind of ecclesiastical form, it deliberately sets at naught the tradition of Christendom. Yet (in its best days, at least) that Society was so deeply imbued with personal devotion to Christ that within its limits it established a very closely knit and compact community.

This instance shows how hopeless is the task of divesting Christianity of churchliness.

It shows also how vast a difference there is in the ways in which men construe this churchliness.   Does churchmanship mean a share in the whole varied life which has flowed through society since Pentecost, or are men (even while admitting the social nature of their religion) to be concerned mainly to emphasise their difference from the ages that are gone, and condemn as superstitious every custom which has against it the caprice of the hour?

Now the truth which, I believe, tends more and more to establish itself, as we study at once the history of religion and the facts of the world to-day, is that the Christian Church is at the centre of the re-ligious experience of the human race.   She is the home of the soul.   Modern investigation shows how she has gathered up into herself customs from many sources.   That we are, in the truest sense, the heirs of the Jewish Church will be disputed by no one who holds to the Messianic mission of our Lord; indeed, this is our meaning when we call Him Christ Jesus, however much this be forgotten.   Despite the scorn of the Anti-Semites, men still find the Old Testament a

richer treasury of spiritual insight and devotion than any other religious literature
except its sequel.   Our liturgy is steeped
in its phraseology, and it colours our imagination more, probably, than we know.[1]

But this is not all.   We have lately been

[1] On the fact that the Christian Church is the development
of the Jewish, see Dr. Goudge's valuable book, *The Mind of
St. Paul*. "To St. Paul Christianity is no new religion; it is
"simply the old religion, with all its promises fulfilled, or on the
"eve of fulfilment, through Messiah's coming. 'How many
"soever be the promises of God, in Him is the yea.' Christ
"makes no new promises; God makes no new promises through
"Him; reconciliation, vindication, the outpouring of the Spirit
"—all these things have been promised long ago, and Abraham
"and his seed have always been expecting them. And this old
"religion remains as corporate as it has always been. There is
"no inheriting of God's promise, except by belonging to the
"Israel of God, and being children of Abraham. In the language
"of a later theology, 'Extra ecclesiam nulla salus'; you cannot
"have God for your Father, unless you have the Church for your
"mother. And this Church, be it observed, out of which there is
"no salvation, is not a new Church, but the old Jewish Church.
"St. Paul knows no other. If you are not a member of the chosen
"people of God, you have no share in the salvation promised to
"it . . . I believe that there is one Church, and only one—the
"Church of Abraham and his seed—and that there never has
"been, and never will be, any other." And again: "I do want to
"urge that the distinction we are accustomed to draw is not justi-
"fied by the New Testament, and that it inflicts real loss upon us
"by cutting us off from our glorious spiritual ancestry in the Old
"Testament. The Jewish Church and the Christian Church are
"one; the Jewish Church was ever intended to become Catholic,
"and the Catholic Church is nothing but the Jewish Church come
"to its full stature. Let me begin with a clear example of this.
"The woman clothed with the sun in Rev. xii. is the Church, and
"she is at one and the same time the Jewish Church, who is the

told that the terminology of St. Paul owes much to the mystery cults of the Roman Empire. All that we learn serves to bring into clearer light the uniqueness of the Christian religion. But it is not the uniqueness of a statue fallen from heaven; rather it is that of a tree planted by the water-side, nourished by the dew and rain, and changed by every wind that blows. We need not fear to allow that Christianity was the supreme mystery-cult, and overcame, in the struggle for existence, many others like those of Mithra or Eleusis, and that in this she doubtless assimilated much from the systems all about. So again in that social product, the Liturgy. Like a net cast into the sea, it gathers of every kind, and has won its compelling beauty through the age-long operation of social forces which have been wider than any individual genius, and have united to create a whole which could not

"mother of the Messiah, and the Catholic Church, who is perse-
"cuted after the Messiah's ascension. I do not at all think that
"that is merely a peculiarity of Johannine symbolism. We speak
"indeed continually to-day of our Lord as founding the Church;
"we even speak of its being the purpose of His coming to found
"it. But where does He use such language?" (Pp. 114–116,
120, 121.)

be the work of a single man or even of one generation. In the ritual, and the order, and every accompaniment which has the consecration of time and thereby enables us to worship more deeply, we possess a home of the spirit in which the soul can take her rest. It envelops us like an atmosphere, although in all our use of it we should guard against a spirit merely antiquarian. As I said last week, the Church is the Church of all the ages, not of any one of them; and we, the heirs, must not only use, but also develop, what we inherit.

If this be true of the outward cult of the Church, it is even truer of its thought. Each age has left some mark on the Christian theology. The Church may modify here and develop there; yet she will always be the Church of Athanasius and Basil, of Ambrose and Augustine, and can never be as though they had not lived. This is true—little as the fact is to our taste—not only of the fathers, but of the mediæval scholastics and of the sixteenth-century reformers. Members of the Church, such as St. Thomas Aquinas on the one hand, Luther and Calvin on the other, have pro-

foundly affected her thought. No condemnation will alter this fact. Rome herself is at the moment different—very different—from what she would be, had they
not arisen. Hegel used to say that a man
could no more jump out of his own age
than he could jump out of his own skin;
and it is no less true that he cannot, by any
contempt for the past, jump out of " all the
ages," although we must hold that he himself
adds a real quality. For the development
of the Church is living, not dead,—creative,
not mechanical. Each age does not merely
carry on; it transcends all ages before it.

Once the root fact of sociality in religion
be grasped, and churchliness admitted as a
necessity, there are two possible attitudes
which a man can take up. He may take
the Church's life in all its fulness of development, and, while refusing to be bound
slavishly to the past, determine to lose no
whit of its splendour. Such an one will
look on Churchmen of all time as emphatically a band of contemporaries, and thus
discern that true instinct of the old masters
which caused them to paint St. Dominic,
St. Athanasius, St. Catharine and St. Bernard

as all equally alive, kneeling at the Cross. On the other hand, a man may be conscious mainly of the defects (and these were very real) in previous times, conscious to such an extent that it seems the best course to turn one's back on them, and to take from the past the minimum of instruction.

This latter course, accompanied by that individualism which is rampant now, is that pursued by the Protestant; and it is the former which commends itself to the Catholic spirit. Nor are the names altogether inappropriate. The one suits well a temper of criticism, of dislike of a system just because it is there, of distrust of all tradition; while the other implies a readiness to admit everything that is truly human, if consecrated by the Holy Spirit working in the Church. The one temper will be disposed to dislike any institution or custom, unless it can be immediately justified on the score of utility; the other will be prepared to wait, and, while not denying the power of the Christian society to change, will want very strong grounds for action before it discards any element, whether of practice or theory, that has the sanction of experience. Even although it seems to us out of date or absurd, it is not certain but that the ground of this repulsion may lie rather in us, with our one-sided development, than in the rite itself, which perhaps ministers to some power of the soul, atrophied through lack of nourishment.

Perhaps an analogy will make the difference clear. Take such an ancient custom as academic, or any other official, costume. The temper which we call Protestant would condemn it as useless and out of date;[1] the temper which we call Catholic, will cherish it with reverence, as dignifying life, and expressing its distinctive character, also as attaching us to the long roll of worthies who have worn these robes with their special significance. In social matters, despite the growth of a very real freedom, most people are more, not less, ready than they were a generation ago to admit the value of ancient or distinctive costumes, and of any kind of pageantry that has an appeal to the eye. On that ground, the temper inside the

[1] A characteristic instance of this is found in a lament of Richard Cobden, the mid-Victorian leader of Manchesterism. He deplores the reactionary tendency symbolised by the aldermen of Manchester adopting red gowns of office.

Christian Church, which sets high value on these things, with their power of subtle suggestion, is likely to meet with more and more general approval. Here indeed a caution is needed. This tendency needs to be severely controlled, or there may be the danger of religious worship becoming a dilettante æstheticism.

Let us pass to other matters. Greek thought most certainly had its influence in the earlier stages of Christian theology. This was inevitable. Men could not formulate the doctrine of the Incarnation or of the Trinity except in terms then current; and they were forced to make use of the categories of the day. The creeds of the Church carry with them that note of circumstance. Nor, again, is it hard to see that, as expressions of the great fact, they are not perfect. It is a pity we have, so many of us, forgotten that the proper term for the formula of belief is *symbol*. The point to ask, then, is not whether they are perfect, but whether they are expressive. Do they symbolise what both we and their authors mean by the great supernatural fact of the Christian religion? Supposing we were to remodel

them to-day in accordance with our prevailing fashions, should we obtain results
that would, after a century, seem any better?
If we feel that these venerable statements
are a real expression of that fact of which
I spoke last time, we shall make no trouble
about loyalty; for we shall deem it wiser
to live in a society which bears, in every part
of its life, the mark of genuine experience,
than to construct some purely schematic
religious institution, adequate as it may seem
to this time, but for that reason adequate to
no other.

All this depends on two conditions.
First, that the Church of Christ, if not
verbally infallible, is at least always so far
inspired by His Spirit that she will not
altogether belie her Founder; and secondly,
that there is in her presentment through the
ages sufficient unity and continuity to make
it a worthy aim to retain as much as may
be of the riches of her life. We, of our
Church, claim that, so far as the Church is
Catholic, we share that universal heritage,
that we are (or need be) less the creatures
of one particular time or of one intellectual
climate, that no enrichment that is helpful

or venerable need be given up; while we are ever open to new knowledge and ways of life. I am speaking now of ourselves, and how we may justify our own loyalty to a body which, despite all its complacent worldliness, seems to us less subject either to vagaries of mere novelty or the torpor of conservatism than any other. Rome, though great in the riches of her unbroken life, and still powerful and persuasive, appears to rest upon a false conception of government, derived from the pagan empire; to be provincial in her development, while claiming universality; and to be tied to a legalist notion of authority which is less and less tenable. She reflects that phase of mediæval life in which men could ignore all Christendom but the West; and she seems to be tied to the intellectual methods of the thirteenth century, which, though great and valuable in their own day, are hardly to be deemed final. The Eastern Churches, though without the incubus of the Papacy, have so far not shown themselves alive to the newer knowledge of the world, and seem without that out-giving energy needed so greatly to-day. Not, however, without humility and rever-

E

ence should we approach them; for it is probable that we have far more need to learn therefrom than we have hitherto been apt to suppose. The various Protestant bodies, until recently, either repudiated or minimised any connection with their spiritual ancestry; and, although they have preserved more of the life than at one time they would have liked to admit, yet they still (even when they consist of baptized Christians) have clinging to them too much of the air of a single epoch to make them a desirable spiritual home for those who seek for a religion, not of one, but of all the centuries. Where indeed they retain the Evangelical Faith, they are best regarded as sections or guilds of the Catholic Church, which set small store by certain parts of the universal cult, and suffer correspondingly.[1] Much, however, of the most modern Protestantism is without these characteristics. It is either purely an ethical system, or a "new theology" which is Pantheism in everything but the name, and can have no faith in that gift which we considered last time. Church-

[1] I say nothing as to the question of the validity of their official representation,

men like you have a right to feel that, in
its insistence on the true ministry, its value
of the sacraments and tradition, our part of
the Church has been wise in clinging to the
order which has come down, while it is freer
than any other from the petrifaction of
mere conservatism, and can make trial of all
the avenues of new experience.

This churchmanship, however, must be
Catholic, not provincial.   We must not
refuse to learn from the fervour and evangelical zeal of those bodies which sit loose
to our system.   Still more must we beware
of applying to the twentieth century and its
needs standards or methods fitted only for
the sixteenth, or even the seventeenth.
We must be prepared to go to school to
the Middle Ages for much devotion, though
keeping away from mere superstitious accre-
tion.   We must not be surprised to find in
other churches, both in the East and the
West, many elements and aspects of spiritual
life which we have for long been content to
lack ; and we must apply what we learn.
A mere provincial Anglicanism is no religion
wherewith to convert the world, pleasing
though it be to the historical sentimentalist

dwelling in the Caroline climate, or expressive of the nice proprieties of ancient country towns. Nor, again, do we want a mere Gothic revival Christianity : though perhaps at this moment the danger is no longer there. If the Church be what we claim that she is, Catholic, the true and universal home of the spirit of man, we must beware of any view of her which would crystallise her life at any moment, either of the past or the present; and we must see to it that our boast is justified that in her the spiritual treasures are richer, freer, and more varied than in any other society. People talk sometimes of an ecclesiastical atmosphere as stifling. Certainly it need not be so ; but is it not sometimes our fault which makes them think that it is ?

All this, however, will not pass without challenge. It is indeed deeply despised by many who bear the name of Christian. One such instance I may notice. Some little time ago a sensation was made in Germany, and in a less degree later on in England, by a work entitled in its translated form, *The Foundations of the Nineteenth Century*. The author, Mr. Houston Stewart

Chamberlain, who married a daughter of
Wagner, is a Germanised Englishman of
intense conviction and wide reading, alike
in philosophy and natural science, and apparently in many other subjects too. Of this
there can be no doubt to anyone who gives
himself the pains to read the thousand
pages of his book; nor, again, can there be
any question of his real independence of
mind or powers of acute criticism. The
writer's desire is to lay the foundations of a
Christianity which shall be the religion of
the future. Moreover, his method is in this
sense truly historical, that he takes the
nineteenth century as the starting-point,
and then makes a regress through universal
history to explain it—which is the method
which, earlier in this lecture, I gave reasons
for approving. The result of his inquiry
is briefly this: the author is confirmed in a
view of life which he himself regards as
Christian, and is equally contemptuous of
all the forms in which hitherto this spirit
has been manifested, with a partial exception in favour of German Protestantism.
While he preserves intact the one compelling figure of Christ, the author manages

to convey the impression that everything
else in the history of Christianity has been
a mistake, except when it was a crime.
Judaism is to him mere idolatry; and he
stigmatises as materialist all the character-
istically Israelitish beliefs in a transcendent
God, a created world, a historically concrete
revelation, and all alleged miraculous occurrences. Our Lord Himself was not Jewish
at all, for the Galileans were mostly of
alien blood. The Greek metaphysics which
got into the creeds, and even the fourth
Gospel, are so inadequate as to be false.
Even greater is the writer's scorn for all
that came down from the Roman Empire
—that chaos of mongrel races; for race
is to him the one supreme fact, and
humanity is nonsense. Sacramental mysticism is Egyptian in origin, and of no greater
worth than the rites of Astarté. The only
force that can make Christianity what it is
meant to be comes from the Teutonic conquering race—" the splendid blonde beast "
of Nietzsche. Luther began the work of
freeing the spirit; even he, however, was
overmuch chained to Catholic dogma. Kant
is the originator of the real liberating

movement, which in the future will develop into a vigorous Teutonic Christianity. Meanwhile it is vain to talk of the Catholic religion, or of the spiritual progress of humanity. Humanity does not exist. There are only races. Mongrel peoples, such as those descended from the slave-population of the Roman Empire, are not to be counted, except in so far as affording evidence against any doctrine or practice which they adopt. Jews, indeed, are an unmixed race, but they are Semites, and Semites can be no guide to Aryans. The Teutons alone hold in their grasp the torch of the world's enlightening. For them a Christianity, redeemed from dogma, cult, and sacrament, will regenerate the conquering powers of earth ; and for the rest she will " bind their kings in chains, and their nobles with fetters of iron."

This book was greatly over-praised. Few will have sympathy for certain of the more extravagant dicta of the writer—such as his theory of the non-Jewish parentage of our Lord, and of the Teutonic origin ascribed to Dante, St. Augustine, St. Paul, and indeed every historical character whom the author happens to like. For all that, Mr. Chamberlain is not to be lightly contemned. He expresses, in striking form and with some persuasive power, ideas which ferment to-day in many minds. Why should the Christians of the twentieth century be tied to the apron-strings of Athanasius? Why should they go to school to St. Ambrose and St Augustine? Why not forget the past of the Church, and start on the quest unre-garding? Is there any real sense in talking of a universal Church, of the spiritual home of humanity, and so forth? Is there very much ground for talk of the progress of mankind, as distinct from the limited and specialised development of small sections? If so, what becomes of the notion of a Catholic Church? Might it not be truer to say that Churches are real, but the Church—One, Holy, Catholic, Apostolic—is a dream, un-less it be a nightmare? It is vain to con-temn this attitude as mere pert provincialism. All of us, in our heart of hearts, are aware that much has gone which can never come back, and that we are far removed from the mental habit of the ages when the New Testament was written, or of that in which the creeds were shaped and the Christian liturgies were elaborated, or of the century which fought over Justification by faith, or that in which Puritanism succumbed beneath its own triumph.

The answer to the genuine difficulty of which such books as this are the expression appears to be twofold:

(1) The gibe would hold good, provided the Catholic conception of the Christian Society means the reign of the dead; and it is good as against those who so interpret it. Nemesis is overtaking those teachers and priests who subsist on the dry bones of a dead tradition.   One can find Churches preening themselves on their Catholic heritage, while in reality they have nothing to show but an arid legalism, unless it be a yet more futile antiquarianism. We can use the Catholic vision to our profit only as we interpret it to mean the power of a living Church to free all the elements that come down to it, to reinterpret and transcend the past; all other use of them will land us in disaster. As against those who appeal merely to tradition, the modern Roman Catholic is more than justified in claiming

the "living" spirit of the Church. Nietzsche in one of his most illuminating essays has shown the danger of all modern culture, that it makes men feel like epigoni living on the past—the end of an age.[1]

The past may help us, but we are to live now and hereafter. Belief in the Catholic Church is belief in development; and this means a creative evolution, not, as some would have it, a development which came to a stop at some moment, which indeed varies according to taste, but at any rate was past before any of us were born. Let all of us who value our inheritance, and set great store by the treasure that has come down to us through the tears and prayers of un-counted saints, remember this; what they give us is not an outward thing, like a precious stone, hard and changeless, but a life, a spirit. Bearing always in mind that the two thousand years of Church history are but the beginning, and that if we are not to say that the age of Chrysostom and Augustine and Bernard was the era of "the rattle and the bottle," we shall pay them

[1] See "The Use and Abuse of History," in *Thoughts Out of Season*.

the truest reverence by doing our part in ministering to the needs of the Church in face of the world we live in, using without capitulation every help that comes from experience.

(2) On the other hand, when we are invited, on the strength of certain dubious theories, to repudiate that experience, and to try an entirely fresh start, we reply first, that this is impossible, and, secondly, that such a proceeding, if not impossible, would be blasphemy—a denial of God's Providence, and of the whole meaning of a historical religion. Are we to believe that, though the gates of hell are not to prevail against the Church, yet its whole scheme, alike of thought and practice, of worship and sacrament, the doctrines of the Incarnation and the Atonement, are to go for nothing, while still we are to call ourselves Christians? Such a view of history would need absolute demonstration before a wise man could accept it; and, so far from its being demonstrated, the contrary can be seen to be very probable.

The test of a system as a whole is richness of life and the type of character it tends to honour. The test of the Christian

Church is the lives of the saints ; only we must include in that term a wider range than is often imagined. " A man is known " by the company that he keeps. In its " human relations, and apart from an explicit " account of its faith concerning the realm " of the gods, or concerning God, a religion " can be justly estimated only when you " understand what kinds and grades of " human beings it bids you recognise." [1]

Those of our adversaries who tell us that the ideal of the Christian character is false and unnatural, are on their own premises right. So long as people admire that character, so long will they manage to find grounds for their loyalty to that society in which alone it can flourish. The supreme apologetic for large numbers of people is this ; they will believe in the religion which makes such and such a character possible. Experience has shown at last that the Christian character, although never perfectly attained, has in it a certain unique quality ; that this cannot, except in very exceptional cases, be produced, even in appearance, in an alien society. Owing to the increase of our

[1] Royce, *o.c.*, vol. i. p. 164.

knowledge of the social atmosphere of other religions and to the growth among us of groups very much aloof from Christian living, we are better able than our fathers to realise this unique quality. Therefore the problem is set to every man, " What think ye of Christ ? "

No force of argument can be decisive here. Those to whom the character of " Jesus " makes no appeal are not likely to be persuaded, even though one rose from the dead. At the same time, it must be said that the appeal of the Christian ideal takes many forms. The Christian Church is the Body of Christ, the expression, in time, of His Spirit. The appeal of Jesus is discerned by some only in the poor man of Nazareth; others may see it clothed with the garments of times more like their own ; or they may find its chief attraction not in any single one, but in the variety and splendour of its manifestations. In any and every case, however, the appeal, in some form, is made to the compelling beauty of the concrete examples of Christian living. In any and every age, and with every individual, there is always some ideal which he would like to resemble

—even if it be that of a company-promoter.
We used, as children, to be taught to say,
" I want to be an angel"; although indeed
we most of us desired nothing of the sort.
But the ideal of Christlike aspiration which
the writer meant was true enough. No
race, no culture, no individual is exempt
from this choice. In all time some there
will be who will reply, " Not this man, but
Barabbas." On them too will come, as on
those who first said it, the Nemesis which
they themselves invoked, " His blood be
on us and on our children."

For the question concerns not merely the
individual, but civilisation as a whole. Is
our civilisation turning its back on Christ?
I do not say certainly that it is; yet many
indications point that way. If they are
correct, and if they are not hereafter
counteracted, then civilisation, in any form
which one can honour, is doomed beyond
recall; " for the wages of sin is death; but
"the free gift of God is eternal life in Christ
" Jesus our Lord."

III

NEWNESS OF LIFE

"If any man be in Christ, he is a new creature." (2 Cor. v. 17.)

NEWNESS of life was the poignant experience of the first Christians. The sense of freshness, of hitherto unknown levels of being, which comes into every lover pervades the whole thought of St. Paul, and in some form or other has been the mark of every vital era in the history of the Church.

The problem before the Church to-day is to prove to men that this is still true of us. While loyal to all those institutions that enshrine the piety and wisdom of ages, cherishing every living element, every phrase, every gesture in the cult and worship that is ours by inheritance, we must not rest in these things, but must make our own contribution to the temple of God, and hand on the torch, aflame with faith, to them that come after.

Truly indeed, as I said last time, we do

well to wonder at the electing Providence which has bestowed on us so beautiful a home, so that we enter into the fruits of the labours of many centuries, and enjoy the vineyards we did not till. In religion, no less than in other forms of social life, national, educational, and professional, a great living tradition is the noblest of all inheritances. Mere conceit it is which would set little store by the achieved heritage of the past. About the Church of our fathers there clings that touch of pathos that belongs to all things that have long sheltered the thoughts and lives of men; and when to this we add the sense that here man has felt himself close to God, he who would remain unmoved must have a nature less than human. This beauty in its purest form is symbolised by some English country church shadowed by yews and set in its landscape of meadows looking towards gentle hills in a blue distance, with its memories of many worshippers. Yet we must not let it bind us by a spell. Mere historic sentiment is not enough for a living religion; nor is it even necessarily Christian. Even a sense of the vital import of Christ and the

Church, "against which the gates of hell shall not prevail," will have no force to win the heart of the twentieth century, if it only come before men as a copy of the Christianity of the sixth, or the thirteenth, or the sixteenth century. A Gothic revival religion will not suffice for a world which is aflame for what is new, and has little place, even in art, for antiquarian sentiment. We cannot live at second-hand; and echoes, even of church bells, will not redeem us.

Newness is the essence of the age we live in. The twentieth century is very young, and very conscious that it is not the nineteenth. It has the exuberance and a little of the arrogance of youth, but it has also its charm. Unless we can minister as Churchmen to this passion for the freshness and breath of reality, it will be all in vain that we shall tell it of the massive powers of Christian tradition, of the greatness of the fathers, or even of the glories of saints and martyrs. It is not the splendour of the past, it is the splendour of the future that men are crying for; and we must show them that we have the secret thereof—we and none other. All the considerations of

F

which we spoke last time are a drawback rather than an advantage to that temper of adventure which is now so prevalent and is not unhealthy. The world has awakened out of slumber, and cries out upon the futile irrelevancies that have done duty for thought, and demands reality. Can we satisfy this curious age that this reality is to be found in Christ Jesus, and that, even as a matter of interest, the Christian has a fuller life than anyone else? Or is the Church merely to exist as a body of "pensioners on the past," sheltering those who prefer to live by an ancient tradition, or the *dilettanti* who breathe by preference any atmosphere but that of their own age? What is the use of persuading people that the Church is the home of the soul, if their one object is to leave that home behind them and seek fortunes afar?

Faced by such doubts, the first thing we should answer is that no novelty in outward circumstance can change the fundamental being of man, and that religion is no less needful to him than love or activity. Neither evolution, nor the triumph of mechanical skill, nor the enlargement of the historic vision have altered the fact that man is a being who chooses, who loves, and who sins. If, and in so far as, the Christian Church ministers to man in his freedom, his struggles, his affections, and his failures, it must retain its power over his life. That will be so, even though some may lose sight of the reality in the appearances, or, through concern with the outward concomitants of existence, have become ignorant of life.

Even, however, with this reply, we have still to persuade men that the Church is a source of life and power, and not a petrified obstruction. Men are not wrong in asking to be satisfied that the Christian Church has a future as well as a past; nor are they altogether wrong when they suspect that she has not. If they are misled, it is partly the fault of the Church. Too often has Christianity become identified with mere tradition or outward respectability. Too often it is treated, not as a living spirit, but as a dead deposit. Much even of genuine piety is so hidden behind a conservatism of convention that it is not easy for an outsider to disentangle it.

But we do not make the antiquity of its

institutions a ground for denying the vitality
of a people ; nor do we find, in length of
inherited tradition, grounds for denying the
powers of immediate development. Why
need we do so in regard to the Church? It
is clear that any society must, after a brief
period, develop forms, ways of acting, and
expression. Is there in Church history any
ground for supposing that these developed
forms have clogged her life, or that from a
living power she has become a dead establishment? Every reason there has been in all
ages to suspect that she was in danger of
this decadence, and no reason to say that
she has not escaped it; *i.e.* if at any moment
he looks at the spectacle of the Church, an
outside observer might be pardoned for thinking that amid all this officialdom, routine,
ritual, law, dogma, formula, and the active
and positive worldliness, and even unbelief,
of many, the life of the religion was at
an end. Only, this has never been the case.
No institution known to history has shown
such amazing powers of recuperation as the
Christian Church; nor has any shown such
powers of adaptation to fresh conditions.
Her transformation by St. Paul from a sect

of Judaism to a universal religion was probably unthinkable to the earliest Christians; her conquest of the barbarian races was doubtless beyond the vision of many, even in the age of St. Augustine; while, even to those who took part in them, the Cluniac and Hildebrandine revival in the eleventh century, the Franciscan development with its *insperata novitas* in the thirteenth, the conciliar movement in the fifteenth, and the changes specially entitled the Reformation in the sixteenth, must all of them have seemed almost too good to be true before they actually took place. Strangest of all is the recovery after the eighteenth century. That is the period which we ought always to study when we are tempted to depression; for in the eighteenth century was felt the full effect of the Renaissance, together with the development of the doctrine of natural law and the result of the schisms of Western Christendom. The coldly critical rationalism, everywhere triumphant, in that day condemned with its superficial scorn the history and the hopes of Christians alike, and in the imposing establishments of national religion saw nothing but

a toppling order, as many do now. Even
where a nominal faith was retained, it had
to pay toll to the *Zeitgeist*, and whittled
down the Christian creed to a vague belief
in God as supreme governor, and Christ as
the prophet of natural religion, coupled with
some sense of the value of religion for
public order. Never since the earliest times
of Christianity has the mind of educated
Europe been so openly and universally contemptuous of Christian belief as it was in
the era of the "enlightenment." Bolingbroke and his congeners here, or, abroad, the
followers of Voltaire, looked forward with
certainty to the speedy downfall of the
Christian Church; and the general attitude
of the polite world was described in words
that have become classical in the preface to
Butler's *Analogy.* Verily religion seemed
at its nadir. Yet we know the startling
revival, and all the strange developments of
the nineteenth century,—how alive she
showed herself in learning, in research, in
the revival of the sacramental side of
Christianity, in the very institutions, like
"religious life" and ascetic self-denial,
which to the eighteenth century seemed

as dead as the Gothic churches which it despised.

The men of wit and taste of the days of Bolingbroke and Warburton and Horace Walpole and Lady Mary Wortley Montagu would have rubbed their eyes indeed could they have seen the Church life of the days of Pusey and Liddon, of Lightfoot and Westcott, and Creighton and Gore. Still more would they have felt surprise at its developments in this country.

But, after all, it is said that these revivals are in the past. Nobody denies that the Christian spirit has constantly renewed its youth like the eagle; no one is afraid to question its services to civilisation in the past because, like the Positivist, he holds that the era is at an end. The whole question is whether the impulse is not now exhausted, whether the revival of the nineteenth century was not the last flicker of a dying fire.

Now it is clear that these instances do not prove anything about the present or about the future; but at least they give pause to our thought before we yield to clamour. We must not allow ourselves to be hypnotised into admitting that there is no hope

of converting men to Christianity because
Christian belief is no longer possible to
a certain number of intellectuals, a class
conditioned by certain social and economic
developments not likely to last.   Moreover, whatever may be true of the others,
one instance—viz. that of the eighteenth
century—is germane to the present issues.
The intellectual collapse then was far more
universal than it is now, and the prospects
of the Church all over Europe were darker.
The grounds on which men denied the
foundation facts and truths of the Gospel
were believed to be more secure, by a larger
proportion of instructed people, than any of
those we see to-day.   Men thought that
the human mind was able to demonstrate
the impossibility of all the doctrines of
Christianity that are really distinctive.
Such sweeping judgments are, however,
now far less general than they were wont to
be.   Daily new realms of possibility open
before man.   Moreover, many studies, not-
ably those connected with psychical phenomena, have rendered narratives credible
which a few years back would have been
scouted, except by the common people.

Still it is said there is one difference. Unbelief in earlier ages was unscientific, but Darwin changed everything. As a matter of fact, unbelief in the eighteenth century was no more and no less unscientific than it is now. Apart from that, we are free to admit that our sense of development of the whole world as a history has become more acute. This, among other things, entails the knowledge of the relative brevity of the Christian epoch; two thousand years of life is a much smaller thing than it was to our fathers. Also, we know a great deal more about its relation to other religions. Meanwhile the mechanical notion of evolution finds less and less to say for itself. The advent of M. Bergson (whose knowledge of science makes him a sure guide where many philosophers are of no help) has meant the breaking down of the terror caused to many by the notion of progress, and the insertion of freedom—creative activity—into the story of the world. Not that his system is necessarily Christian, still less that he denies evolution. On the contrary, he asserts it more thoroughly than do any of his predecessors; but it is a real, living development, not the mere unwinding of a watch. Consequently, there is room for unique events, new beginnings; which is what we mean by miracle. Clearly, moreover, such an event as the miraculous birth of Christ falls in with this scheme naturally enough, if we think of a new creation as beginning there. The view of Bergson, the growth of vitalism, and other more general causes, such as the restoration of a belief in real freedom—all tend to make it less difficult than it was ten or twenty years back to hold to the facts of the Christian story.

But many deny it. Of course they do. The ground of the existing situation is the gradual development of religious liberty. Unless toleration is to be a mere name, it is obvious that it must mean the open rejection of Christian belief by many who in other ages would have been silent. Many men and women in all ages refuse to direct their lives by the Christian ideal. Where this is so, and where they are sufficiently educated, they will be certain to throw off an outward allegiance which has ceased to affect their life. It is only a half-educated world, or an unfree society, which tolerates lives lived in practical repudiation of Christ while faith is apparently unchanged. Moreover, many others in an age like this, even if desirous of belief, may find it impossible; and, since there are now no reasons for disguise, all this produces an exaggerated appearance of shrinkage. With the advent of real toleration, conventional religion must decay. Only those with eyes fixed on the seventeenth century, when Christianity was coextensive with citizenship, are really deceived by this. Toleration was bound to turn Christendom into a mere section of mankind. In regard to the life of the Church, the question is not whether she is including, or is likely to include, a majority of the population, but whether the life that burns inside her members is strong or weak. Those who, either in sorrow or scorn, point at the decay of Church membership would sing a very different song if they could realise the terrific intensity of Church life in quarters the most unlikely, and the strides she makes, despite many odds, in the crowded centres of our great cities. We must beware of attributing to an increased weakness of the Christian spirit a condition which is the natural and inevitable result of toleration.

Still, however, we are not rid of the difficulty. Is there any quality inherent in Christianity which has the promise of this exhaustless fertility, without which it cannot endure? I think that there is. In the first place, the whole meaning of the Christian religion is that it looks beyond this life for its fruition, and that it does not believe in any perfection this side the grave; thus it can never (while remaining Christianity) realise a condition of equilibrium. All the schemes for the amelioration of human life which are limited to this world, must be theoretically capable of entire realisation, and so far may be exhausted. There comes a time—in thought at least—when the social reformer must sit down and weep with Alexander, for there are no new slums to conquer. John Stuart Mill, in a moving passage of his autobiography, has told us of the melancholy that came over him as he contemplated the possible accomplishment of the hopes of human improvement on which he set such store. He felt that, even when privilege and corruption were done away and injustice remedied and the oppression of the poor a dream gone by, the spirit would still be unsatisfied; and a great weariness overwhelmed him. Now, what Mill felt was due, not to a temperamental weakness, but to a flash of insight into the Nemesis that dogs the steps of all reformers who set their affections on things below. Realisation may be distant, but it is not inconceivable; and, when in conscious thought we face the other side of realisation, the soul rises in rebellion, refusing to be comforted, for that " God created man to be immortal, and made him an image of His own eternity."

With the Christian this weariness has no place. So long as men set before them, not the perfection of terrestrial existence, whether in State or family or individual, but the development of the soul by the process of an endless life, so long have they that in front which leaves them ever restless and unsatisfied.

In this regard there is seen the capital importance of keeping in sight the other-worldly aim in Christian living. If for an

hour we allow ourselves to become im-
mersed in any scheme of Christian progress
that is confined purely to this world, we
shall find, not merely that we have lost our
true character and distinction, but also that
the spring and vitality of all our work is
gone.   Only as we live within the circle
of the Ascended Glory shall we be really
able for work here.   It is they that wait
on the Lord who renew their strength;
they, and they alone, whose hearts are in
the eternal world above, are to walk and
not faint, and mount up on wings as eagles.
Mere natural strength, that of the youth,
grows faint and weary, and the confidence
of mankind shall wither and fall; but the
God-intoxicated souls, though weak and
simple, can run and not be weary, can walk
and not faint.

Thus, as it seems to me, Christians, so
long as they are true to themselves, have
within them a spring of exhaustless novelty,
a power of new effort which will break out
when least expected.   So long as Christianity remains Christianity at all, she will
always be able to rise from the ashes of
respectability.   Should, however, Christians

be so foolish as to listen to the voices of some so-called friends, and to deny the other-worldly reference, their religion would at once lose its *élan vital;* it would sink to be one of the many schemes which would be considered at a social science congress, and in all probability would not outlast a century. It is in our vision of the other world that lies the spring of vitality, and all freshness of a new activity in this.

Finally, let us briefly consider some of the signs that now exist among us of the fresh life and energy of the Church.

First of all come the attempts, varied and by no means always successful, to relate the faith of the Church to the results of modern discovery. Modernism, though it is a name for a movement only in the Roman communion, is part of a wide tendency among all thinking men in the Church of God. Modern knowledge is not all of it so secure as some of its exponents proclaim; and it is a false claim that the Western mind, in its present stage of development, is so certain a criterion that anything that seems to contradict it in the story of the Gospel is *ipso facto* ruled out of court.[1] Still less wise is it to take the path chosen by some of the more extreme members of that school, and to give up all that is distinctive in Christianity in the desire to be modern, and to surrender the concrete historical character of the Gospel, the activity and transcendence of God, and so forth. Nevertheless, the problem which the modernists tried to face is real. Changes of a very definite nature have come over our way of thought; and not all of them are transient. While holding fast to the "Eternal Gospel," there is before us in this age the task, not yet accomplished, of adjusting to a theology framed in another intellectual climate, a new view of the Bible, enlarged conceptions of history, and deeper knowledge of the natural world and of the mind of man. "Mediating liberalism"[2] is perhaps the best term in which to describe the attitude of wisdom; for that implies a real reverence

---

[1] *Cf.* on one item in this, the discussion of the Resurrection of our Lord by Dr. Goudge in the *Church Quarterly Review* for January 1914.

[2] The term is used by Miss Petre in *The Autobiography of George Tyrrell*, and describes the position of such men as Mr. Wilfrid Ward; see chapter iv. in vol. ii.

for the heritage that is ours, together with an alert openness to what is new. Do not, however, let us suppose there is no problem, or deny changes which are real.[1]

Other movements there are, more directly practical, but of no less moment. What is to be the outcome of the Student Christian Movement? One thing is certain; it will make a difference. Some of its features we may not like; and what will come out of it, no one just now can tell. But the movement is too large to be ignored, too spontaneous to be despised. Already it is having influence in drawing together Christians who, but for this, are in different camps. Father Kelly's book, *The Church and Religious Unity*, is avowedly the result of it; and that work alone shows what a ferment it is producing in the minds of those who might before have been called the upholders of the rigid Tractarian tradition.

Movements for reunion, of which we have so many, form another instance of the ever fresh life in the Catholic Church. Whether

---

[1] So far as I can see, this attitude of denying the problem is that taken up by Mr. Ronald Knox in his brilliant but unsatisfying work, *Some Loose Stones*.

in the near future they will accomplish much, some will doubt ; still less easy is it to predict how they will effect their object, or what the outward face of the Church will be in the year 2000. For our purpose it is enough to note the fact of their existence, the amazingly wide area of support and interest which they cover, and to compare such an event as the World Missionary Conference, for instance, with anything that was possible a hundred years ago.

Missions, again, are probably the strongest proof of the vitality of the Church and of her faith in herself. Is there in this matter any slackening either of interest or devotion ? Rather, surely, all the signs are of increase— and that in an age when the competition for material advantage is so fierce. Moreover, in the mass movements in India and other signs we see the beginnings of that great reaction of missions upon Western Chris- tendom which is so certain and so sorely needed. For there can be little doubt that with the development of Eastern Christi- anity there will gradually come a new spirit into the whole, and that we of the West shall begin to lose some of our hardness and lack of devotion. We shall see more mystics, more ascetic life, and more real devotion in prayer and sacrament. Errors indeed may be made. That "decisive hour" of which Mr. Mott speaks seems rather doubtful. Still, even though some lay too much stress on the chances of the hour, they would not do this were there not a great rush of energy in the Church. If at times we feel depressed by the supercilious scorn of many of the intellectuals, we shall do well to bear in mind that the strength of Christianity lies in the depths of the spirit, and that mere intellectual ingenuity is often sadly to seek in this; and that now more than ever are there signs of the fresh springs of devotion, all over the Church and in every class.

Every class! The Church of the future, if she is to exist at all, must in no way be the appanage of a class. Not merely must she not be a mainly clericalist institution, but she must be a real communion of saints, the body of Christ, in which there is neither Greek nor Jew, male nor female, barbarian, Scythian, bond nor free. How are we going to behave to all those classes which

in all but name are bond slaves, and in
many ways are worse off than if they were
legally so ? Unless we can be the Church
of the poor, we had far better cease to be a
Church at all. Yet here again there are signs
of life. More and more evidence is there that
the conscience of Churchmen is beginning
to be touched. Here indeed is the distinctive difference between our own day and
that of the Evangelicals or of the early Tractarians. Both of these were willing to work
and do their best for the poor; but neither
can be said to have been in any way obsessed
by the appalling horrors of modern industri-
alism, with its accentuated machinery of
oppression, its tolerated hypocrisy, and the
lies and shams of commercial competition.[1]
Now, however, all that is changed or changing. More and more does it appear that no
correctness of dogma, no beauty of Catholic
ritual, no sentiment of devotion, no piety
esoteric and aloof can secure the Church
from collapse, unless she gain a " change of
heart" in regard to the relations of wealth
and poverty. Not indeed that it is necessary, or even desirable, that the Church as a

[1] In this respect Pusey was more modern than Newman.

17958

Church should have a policy; for in the
modern State, which is nothing if not heter-
ogeneous in religion, no policy can be recommended merely on Christian grounds; and
the Church *qua* Church knows of no other.
But the Church as a corporate society ought
to do the deepest penance for her share in
producing the existing relations between
the fortunate classes and the disinherited;
and also for the widespread opinion, which
must have some foundation, that she repre-
sents the cause rather of the rich than of the
poor.   Also, the lax conscience of each individual Churchman and Churchwoman
needs arousing.   Many devout persons, in
matters of income-tax, dutiable goods, and
so forth, are not above descending to
methods which in a shoeblack would have
an ugly name.   Many more are content to
judge every proposal of social improvement
by its probable effect on their dividends, and
to believe that the one purpose of Church
and State is to keep up this rate of interest.
The recent Putumayo revelations, in which
the one shareholder who protested some
years back was threatened with libel, shows
the way in which the investing classes are

willing to get their income.[1] Even apart
from this, and from what we are told of the
methods of high finance as practised by
Christians, how many Christian people have
any notion that they ought to teach their
children a different standard of expenditure
from that of the world ? For clothes, amuse-
ments, expensive meals, motor-cars—indeed,
all forms of self-indulgence—are placed at
the disposal of the young; and they are not
even trained to give away in charity. If
we would only teach the communicant
members of the Church that avarice is a
deadly sin, and that as Christians we are
to be content with food and raiment, we
should have gone half-way to solve the
economic problem; for the energy thus set
free would seek an outlet, and the higher
standard would alter all social life. All
this, however, is changing for the better.
Much remains to be done, and worldliness
will never be eradicated until man is perfect;

[1] The report, it must be remembered, does not confine itself to
condemning foreigners, but shows the responsibility of the
directors. The whole thing is an instance of the logical results
of that greed for gold which is now preached as a religion. *Cf.*
also the remarks of Mr. Justice Darling on the responsibility of
Lipton's directors in the canteen case.

still, there are signs that the confusion of
the Church with an upper and middle-class
sect is beginning to vanish. If it does not
vanish, we are doomed, and rightly doomed.
Errors probably lie before us, and we may
stumble on hard paths; but I cannot for
the life of me understand why Christian
people of this day should have such a
nervous fear of error when it comes to
siding with the poor—in this back-slum
scrimmage which we call "civilisation"—
while it was the danger of subserviency to
the rich that seems to have inspired the
Epistle of St. James.

Let us ask ourselves, in all sincerity,
whether the Christian Church at the present
day exhibits the spirit of St. James, or that
which he so deeply condemns? Can any of
us honestly say that there is no truth in the
exaggeration of Mr. Bernard Shaw, that
"all religious organisations have sold themselves to the rich"?

Easy indeed it is for expensive ecclesi-
astics who have lived all their life in comfortable and highly paid posts, away from
the sorrow and sin of life, to throw scorn on
any poorer clergy who are trying to help the

cause of the poor, or to imply that any effort
of the law to improve their lot is a bandits'
raid on the well-earned remuneration of company promoters. Easy is the task of well-
endowed academic or cathedral officials
whose whole life has been dependent on
the sheltered luxury provided by generous
donors away from ugliness and squalor, to
manipulate the figures in Whittaker, and to
establish the thesis that the comfortable
classes have done all, and more than all,
that can be expected. Yet even these
"whips and scorns" of dons, and the "insolence of office" would not thus throw
scorn on the poor, were it not that the conscience is beginning to speak, and shows its
first stirrings in biting irritation. *E pur si
muove.*

Finally, and this is what I have come
here to say to you, it all rests with us.
Only the event can show whether this
power of life really exists within the church;
she will be what we choose to make her.
What are you going to do?

Are you going to sit still, content to enjoy
without fighting, resting in this home of
beauty raised by the blood and tears of

saints, and furnished with the splendour of prayer and the richness of two millenniums' effort? In that case you may nourish your historical sentiment and even your private devotion, and help a little band of *illuminati*, untouched by the modern spirit; but the glory will have departed. Afraid to face the new forces and to embrace the living hearts of men and women, you cannot hallow their lives; from being indifferent, they will become hostile; and your name and place will be done away.

But you will not do this. This new spirit of the twentieth century is ours—ours for the winning. The spirit of freedom now abroad, with all its eager confidence and loving hope, can meet its true leader only in Jesus Christ. That cry for beauty in life and joy can be met only in the Catholic Church with her age-long heirlooms of service, and the pearl of great price—a Divine love. For it is love that this child-heart of our day is crying out for. Doubtless many faults can be seen in it. The age is trying, like boys and girls, wayward and conceited—but always lovable. Yet once more we have a world on fire with a quest—the quest for adventure, for reality and joy. That adventure can be had in its fullest only by those who are to scale, not the Alpine heights, but the gates of heaven; the reality it can have only in Him Who is the Way, the Truth and the Life. Ours it is to have learnt the secret; ours it is to offer it to the strange piteous world stained with sin, wearied in the greatness of its way, and tossed in the tempest of its own freedom; ours to show it the haven where it would be, the goal of all striving, the end of every man's desire—God's love in Christ Jesus our Lord. Once more we are to make vivid to men who disregard them these words, "Come unto Me, all that travail and are heavy laden, and I will give you rest."

Of course it is hard. To sift from the mass of modern notions what is to be enduring, and then to adjust it with the Christian faith; to minister to the desire of new life, while still loyal to the treasure-house of time; to help in the cause of union, while keeping close to our ancient development; to waken the social conscience of our fellows, while guarding against hatred and malice; even to keep our faith amid the blare in our

ears of ten thousand trumpets of denial—
assuredly the task is hard, almost impossible.
That is why it is worth trying. It is only
the impossible that is worth attempting.
We must live dangerously, said Nietzsche.
Nowhere is this truer than in religion. As
our Lord said, we must lose our lives to
save them; and at no time has this been
truer than now. We have to give "all for
all." And if we do, perhaps we too shall win
the world, or part of it, to see that truth.

IV

SELF-DEVELOPMENT

"I am come that they might have life, and that they might have it more abundantly." (St. John x. 10.)

No quality of Christianity is more arresting than that of life. The abounding vitality of St. Paul, of St. Augustine and of many another leader is doubtless partly physical, and would have shown itself under any conditions. But many members of the Christian society, even in its earlier days, cannot have had more than average powers; and yet it is as a new life, increasing all the energies and doubling men's zest, that the phenomenon of the Christian Church enters upon history. This it is that makes the difference between the beginnings of Christian art and the conventions of dying Paganism. That "conquering new-born joy," which offered a fresh sensation to the world-wearied imperials of Rome, was to these men so rich in hope just because it came with the message that life is worth living. This message is for all. The supreme worth of the individual has always been upheld by the Christian Church, even in its most hierarchical phase. The soul has been always held up as the final interest. Neither the fripperies of abundance nor the squalor of the underworld has anything to say to the question that gnaws the heart : What must I do to be saved? No prince, whether one of intellect or of achievement, is so high set that he needs no redemption; no pauper, whether of mind or character, is so low but he may claim it. That is the unshaken gift of the good news, through all the ages and forms of Christendom. Clearly it implies a value set on human life, such as is native to no other system.

> " There is no soul
> But it's unlike all others in the world,
> Nor one but lifts a strangeness to God's love,
> Till that's grown infinite, and therefore none
> Whose loss were less than irremediable
> Although it were the wickedest in the world." [1]

And this abounding life displays itself in joy. Read the New Testament. It is a

[1] W. B. Yeats *The Countess Cathleen.*

pity so few people read the New Testament just as a book without commentary, merely to get the impression. Is there not a sense of joy in the lives both of writers and readers, more intense than anywhere else in literature? At least I do not know where you will meet its like, except in some of the mystics; although the most real poetry makes an approach thereto. Even there, however, it is found at its highest in poetry, like Dante's *Paradiso*, written in the directly Christian spirit, or in Shakespeare, who takes it for granted. You can see the difference if you compare with Goethe's *Faust*, or the great embodiments of the antique ideal. This ecstasy of life is the passion that flamed in the martyrs, and rises to view in the great Gothic cathedrals, and sprang into a thousand forms in the orders of chivalry and religion, in the pageant of Christian worship, and in the vision of the mystics.

Yet it is precisely the lack of this quality which men now lament. Men talk of the "gloomy asceticism of the Catholic Church." They gibe at the inhuman ethics of renunciation. They cast scorn upon the ideal of self-control, and demand freedom for personality to express itself, unregarding of the Philistine insistence on the ten commandments. Much of modern literature—drama, poetry, and fiction alike—seems to be obsessed with these two notions: first, that the spirit of man is free, and has at last come to know it; and, second, that the Christian ethic means the denial of this freedom, and the enslavement of the spirit to an external and cramping authority. Rightly or wrongly, many men and women of high attainments are filled with these notions, and make this ethical divergence a ground of their hostility to Christianity. In truth, what has emerged more than anything else in the controversies of the last fifteen years is the fact of the ethical distinctness of Christianity. It was denied during what we may call the Huxleian epoch. Any Christian who ventured to assert that the ethics of Christians were dependent on their faith and could not maintain themselves apart from it, was regarded as narrow-minded. On the whole, it was taken for granted that approximately the same ethical values would prevail; here and there Christians might differ from non-Christians, but there would be no real or fundamental divergence. As Mr. Neville Talbot puts it with convincing eloquence in his introductory essay on " The Modern Situation," in *Foundations:*—" The gulf between free-thinking, reforming intellectuals and good Evangelicals or Tractarians was not so deep but that they had moral and even religious assumptions in common. They were often united in such mental and spiritual elements as formed foundations for the religious negations of the one party and for the affirmations of the other. . . . For the most part the minds of liberals in early and middle Victorian times were rich in an optimism drawn from a capital of un-criticised assumptions. They were busy with emancipation from the entail of the past ; their battle-cry was ' Liberty.' If pain was involved in the escape from old beliefs and institutions, it was greatly mitigated for them by the conviction that the essentials of true religion and morality were unaffected by it. An energy in emancipation was given to them by—as it were—their ' stance ' upon a rock of belief, if not

in God, at least in goodness as inherent in
the natural order of things.

"Such optimism lay behind their almost
pathetic belief in education as the way of
all salvation. It quickened their impatience
with ecclesiastical dogmas and sanctions.
It gave heart to men in their struggle with
'Hebrew old clothes.' It allowed that
expansion of ethical fervour which, as in
George Eliot, seemed but to increase with
the loosening of her grasp upon distinctively
Christian doctrine. It reappeared in others
in the assumption of the benevolence of
nature to the individual. Here, indeed,
for the heroes of political emancipation, the
upholders of economic orthodoxy, and the
believers in unrestrained competition and
the doctrine of *laisser-faire*, was the very
fulcrum to the lever of nineteenth-century
liberty. Individual man, it was thought,
needed only to be freed from artificial and
traditional restraints, and to be set in a
nature similarly liberated, for it to provide
to each his meat in due season, and for him
to fare as well as he deserved.

"We can gauge the strength of this optimistic reliance upon nature if we observe

H

its reaction upon Darwinism. Though the doctrine of the 'struggle for existence' in itself cut at the roots of the belief in the benevolence of nature to the individual, many were quick to infer from the observation of a continuous upward development in the past added grounds for their general faith in progress for the future. 'Progress,' indeed, was the bottom layer of Victorian assumptions. It still survives among a superior minority that has disencumbered itself of any other convictions." [1]

All this is changed. Nietzsche has helped many to see that the Christian system of life was something distinct and *sui generis*, and caused them to ask themselves how far it had their allegiance as an ideal—apart from all matters of doctrine. Naturally many were honest enough to discern that the Christian scheme of life is precisely what life does not mean for them. Modern drama, which begins with Ibsen, asks very much the same question, even more significantly. Take, for instance, such propagandist literature on the sex question as Eleanor Key's *Love and Marriage*, with its

---

[1] *Foundations* (Macmillan and Co., 1912), pp. 5, 6.

ideal of adultery made impossible through freedom of divorce, or Mrs. W. M. Gallichan's *The Truth about Woman*, with its reiterated flouting of the ideal of chastity. It is idle to ignore these things, or to speak as though our novelists were ruled by the conventions of a past age. Some of us are blamed, because in matters of profound import like theology or ethics, we seek light from literature, and, instead of playing on the academic bowling-green, have ventured to interrogate the novelists and playwrights and poets. But these people are the prophets of the day; and all literature that is worthy enshrines the aspirations of a time.[1] Besides, our young men and young women are fed on these writings. We cannot prevent their reading and talking of them. Needful it seems to be in the highest degree that we should seek to get at the underlying

[1] An article in the *Athenæum* on "The Task of Theology in the Twentieth Century" has the following passage:

"Experts in criticism or comparative religion—and especially "the theological schools of the universities—are, in our judg- "ment, making a great mistake in ignoring the religious "significance of writers like Mr. H. G. Wells and books like "*The Anthology of Georgian Poetry*. One of the first ele- "ments in the equipment of any modern theologian ought to be "a first-hand acquaintance with the popular novels and dramas "of the day."

spirit of this literature, which becomes in an increasing degree prophetic. No student of Mr. Wells or Mr. Shaw or Mr. Galsworthy (not to mention younger writers) will think quite the same things about the world as if he did not read these books —however little he may agree with what is said.

To come then to the charge with which we began—that Christianity is a " doctrine of the Cross." That charge is well founded. " If any man will not deny himself and take up his cross and follow Me, he cannot be My disciple." Not once nor twice does our Lord make it clear that we must give " all for all "; that while He holds for us the pearl of great price, we cannot take the pearl without we pay the price, and that that price is self-surrender. We are to die to live. " He that loseth his life shall save it; he that will save his life shall lose it." That is the frequent maxim of the Master. It is the burden of St. Paul's own experience ; and his power of translating his inward life into pregnant words makes him a good witness. Throughout his letters—and they are letters —we have the constant iteration of this thought, which must have possessed him, or else it would not come out so often, that the joy of the Christian life comes only out of its accepted pain. Somehow or other the mortification, the death of the lusts and appetites are the condition of true life; and mortification cannot be a pleasant process. You know the classical passages in the Corinthians:

" We are troubled on every side, yet not distressed; we are perplexed, but not in despair; persecuted, but not forsaken; cast down, but not destroyed; always bearing about in the body the dying of the Lord Jesus, that the life also of Jesus might be made manifest in our body." (2 Cor. iv. 8–10.)

And again:

" In all things approving ourselves as the ministers of God, in much patience, in afflictions, in necessities, in distresses, in stripes, in imprisonments, in tumults, in labours, in watchings, in fastings; by pureness, by knowledge, by long-suffering, by kindness, by the Holy Ghost, by love unfeigned, by the word of truth, by the power of God, by the armour of righteousness on

the right hand and on the left, by honour
and dishonour, by evil report and good
report; as deceivers, and yet true; as unknown, and yet well known; as dying, and,
behold, we live; as chastened, and not killed;
as sorrowful, yet always rejoicing; as poor,
yet making many rich; as having nothing,
and yet possessing all things." (2 Cor. vi.
4–10.)

All the principles involved in Christian
asceticism are set forth in the Epistle for
Septuagesima:

" Know ye not that they which run in a
race run all, but one receiveth the prize?
So run, that ye may obtain. And every
man that striveth for the mastery is temper-
ate in all things. Now they do it to obtain a
corruptible crown; but we an incorruptible.
I, therefore, so run not as uncertainly; so
fight I, not as one that beateth the air:
but I keep under my body, and bring it
into subjection; lest that by any means,
when I have preached to others, I myself
should be a castaway." (1 Cor. ix. 24–27.)

Precisely the same parallel is used in the
Epistle to the Hebrews (xii. 1):

" Let us lay aside every weight, and the

sin that doth so easily beset us, and let us
run with patience the race that is set before
us "; while the words following, and others
in the same book, make it clear that in the
writer's view our Lord Himself "learned
obedience from the things which He suffered." (*Cf.* also 2 Timothy ii. 9–12.)

Still more clearly is it the burden of the
Apocalypse, with its emphasis on the gift of
the crown of life only to him that over-
cometh, and its glorification of the martyrs.
Not really different is the doctrine of that
work which is sometimes attacked as an
extravagant statement of the ascetic ideal :

" Quid igitur times tollere crucem
    per quam itur ad regnum ?
        In cruce salus
        In cruce vita
        In cruce protectio ab hostibus
        In cruce infusio supernae suavitatis
        In cruce robur mentis
        In cruce gaudium spiritus :
        In cruce summa virtutis,
        In cruce perfectio sanctitatis.
    Non est salus animae nec spes aeternae vitae
            nisi in cruce.
    Tolle ergo crucem tuam et sequere Jesum ;
    Et ibis in vitam aeternam.

Praecessit ille bajulans sibi crucem,
Et mortuus est pro te in cruce:
Ut et tu tuam portes crucem;
Et mori affectes in cruce.
Quia si commortuus fueris;
Etiam cum illo pariter vives.
Et si socius fueris poenae
Eris et gloriae.
Ecce in cruce totum constat
Et in moriendo totum jacet:
Et non est alia via ad vitam et ad veram inter-
    nam pacem;
Nisi via sanctae crucis et quotidianae mortifica-
    tionis.
Ambula ubi vis,
Quaere quodcumque volueris:
Et non invenies altiorem viam supra,
Nec securiorem viam infra,
Nisi viam sanctae crucis.

.   .   .   .   .

Crux ergo semper parata est;
Et ubique te exspectat.
Non potes effugere,
Ubicumque cucurreris:
Quia ubicumque veneris te ipsum tecum portas;
Et semper te ipsum invenies.
Converte te supra,
Converte te infra,
Converte te extra,
Converte te intra,

Et in his omnibus invenies crucem :
Et necesse est te ubique tenere patientiam,
Si internam vis habere pacem,
Et perpetuam promereri coronam."[1]

These final words and those following
make evident the two points which distin-
guish Christian asceticism and make it a
sound philosophy of life. For first the
writer shows that it is not so much a question
of escaping the cross as of the spirit in
which we bear it. The cross, as he truly
says,—*i.e.* trouble—meets us at every turn,
and we cannot escape it. True wisdom
consists in accepting this as a universal fact,
and in finding in it our hope of joy. That
is the sole method of every kind of courage.
Once this spirit be attained, it will be found
that

" The worst turns the best to the brave,
The black minute's at end."

The courageous man does not of necessity
suffer more pain than the coward ; probably
he suffers less ; but he makes his pain, of
whatever kind, bear fruit to him. As the
writer goes on :

[1] *Imitatio Christi*, II. xii.

"Si libenter crucem portas, portabit te
Et ducet ad desideratum finem,
Ubi scilicet finis patiendi erit:
Quamvis hic non erit.
Si invite portas onus tibi facis
Et te ipsum magis gravas:
Et tamen oportet ut sustineas.
Si abjicis unam crucem
Aliam procul dubio invenies,
Et forsitan graviorem.
Credis tu evadere
Quod nullus mortalium potuit praeterire?"

One note runs through all these passages. The death or cross-bearing is not suffering for its own sake; it is death for the sake of life. Pain is to be endured, embraced even, but always as a condition of joy. It is "the method of all transcendence." The ascetic doctrine of Christian living is a matter of means; and the end is always the same—not the loss, but the saving of self. The Gospel does not attempt to explain suffering or to ignore it. It does not say that it is always a punishment for sin; nor, on the other hand, does it say that it is a delusion, or that in this world we can ever escape it. The self-denial which it teaches

---

[1] *Imitatio Christi*, ii. xii.

is self-renunciation as a means of a fuller life. Here is the radical distinction between Christian and Oriental asceticism and all of those forms of Western pessimism which express a similar view. To the Christian the individual life is a thing of glory and of wonder; but it may be enjoyed in its fulness only on this condition, that we give " all for all." A man must endure pain, face death, and risk everything, or he cannot continue to possess even the little that he has. The doctrine of the Cross is the fullest expression of Nietzsche's maxim " to live dangerously." Its final symbol is the passion of the Lord; the agony upon the Cross and the cry of dereliction were the condition of His triumph.

There is the willing offering of the self to all horror, and the courage which faces the loss of all in order truly to possess it. Even Jesus Christ could not offer Himself entirely without the consciousness of supreme loneliness; and only after the Calvary cry did He commend His Spirit to the Eternal Father.

Christianity may seem, in its preaching of self-renunciation, a doctrine of death; but,

in its assertion of the individual immortality
in the Risen Life, it is a doctrine of the
glory of life, far outreaching any other.
Mr. Shaw has accused us somewhere of not
really facing death because we deny it by
the doctrine of the Resurrection; others
again charge us with selfish aims because
we preach an individual life beyond the veil.
The Christian ethic is thus strangely attacked
on two opposite sides. First it is scouted
as preaching self-annihilation and a morality
of renouncement; then it is attacked for
its appeal to selfish motives, in its doctrine
of a life beyond. At least, however, this
latter charge makes it clear how entirely
free is Christian asceticism from the reproach,
so often levelled at it, of being a doctrine of
death, inhuman and unnatural. That is the
character of those systems which assert that
the source of evil is individual existence,
and teach the denial of all desire with the
object of finally extinguishing individuality.
Such systems, even where they may in-
culcate similar outward conduct, are poles
apart from the Christian faith in eternal
life. True, I think it must be allowed that
Christian self-denial has sometimes been

preached in unwise terms. Language has been used by mystics and others, which, if not Pantheistic in tendency, has that appearance. A doctrine of self-sacrifice may be preached which, far from being that of the New Testament, does lead logically to the extinction of the individual. This may be done by a one-sided emphasis on the rights of the Church, or by a false notion of the relation of the individual to the community, such as that entertained by the Jesuits. But that is not Christianity ; and even those who so teach would deny that their doctrine held these implications. A firm faith in the individual life after death is the one certain bulwark against views of Christian ethics which would make it in reality what its adversaries believe it to be—a doctrine not of life, but of death. Let us ever guard ourselves against the temptation to preach even the right and true doctrine of cross-bearing in such extravagant terms as to give it a tone which means, logically, a denial of immortality and, practically, a weakening of the individual conscience.

So far, then, I think we may take it as established that the self-renunciation in-

volved in Christian ethics is no more than
a means to an end; and that the end
remains what it always has been, that of
life, richer and more abundant life, the development of the personality for a society
beyond this world.

But this is not all. Other systems of
ethics may assert that our method is wrong.
The self-denial preached by the Gospel may
be said to be cruel and inhuman, and calcu-
lated—so far from developing the personality
—to stifle its growth. M. Émile Combes,
it is said, objected to what he believed to be
the self-mutilation involved in monastic
ideals. It remains to show that this charge
is unfounded.

So far from the method of Christian discipline being unnatural and inhuman, it is
the method of advance on every side of
human life, and is what makes life best
worth living. The Cross of Christ, and all
that it implies for our imitation, does but
carry farther the maxims that were taught us
in our earliest days. From the elementary
courage of the child, learning not to cry
out when hurt, and taught that if he shrinks
back before every danger he will never get

the best things of life, down to the utter
renunciation of a St. John of the Cross,
there is a series of steps graduated in difficulty, yet nowhere differing in their real
character. St. Paul himself, and the writer
of the Epistle to the Hebrews, were both
well aware of this; otherwise they would
not have compared the ascetic discipline of
the Christian with the training of the arena,
nor given us the comparison between the
corruptible crown of the athlete and the
heavenly diadem. The same is the case
with our Lord's words about counting the
cost.

Let us consider this more in detail. No
advance of any kind is possible in life
except in obedience to the maxim, "who-
soever will lose his life shall save it." Take
the simplest lesson, universally inculcated
by the common judgment of mankind, and
a prime necessity of physical existence in un-
developed civilisations. Courage in bodily
matters, the knightly ideal, means not
merely that since pain is inevitable it must
be endured, but that literally we are to try
to "grin and bear it." "Never," we are all
told, "can you get the most, the best, out

of life, if you will not suffer hardships and
face dangers." In primitive societies this is
taught by necessity. In a highly complex
civilisation some may be artificially sheltered,
and of these some, to their undying regret,
may escape learning the lesson in youth;
for all that, few will doubt that to make
the best of even bodily life some use must
be made of the maxim that lies at the root
of all Christian discipline. Not merely is
no other condition safe; it is not, in the long
run, so full of joy. Compare (to take a
simple instance) an afternoon holiday as it
may be spent by some loafer in a village,
who has never learnt to use his limbs and
can do nothing with his leisure, with the
same time spent by another villager of the
same age on the football field. The one
can do nothing but lean against a gate, and
is bored and ill-tempered; the other may
come home tired, bruised, perhaps with a
slight accident; yet no one doubts with
which of the two the joy in living is most
intense. So it is with the spirit of adventure in all its forms,—from the training of
the athlete to the soldier's fortitude, or the
adventurous energy of the explorer, or of the

airman. This, however, is a commonplace; but I would that those who have learnt it in practice far better than I have could see its bearing on the whole problem alike of progress and of joy in life.

There is a passage in Mr. Chesterton's *Orthodoxy* which brings it out. "Courage is almost a contradiction in terms. It means a strong desire to live taking the form of a readiness to die. 'He that will lose his life, the same shall save it,' is not a piece of mysticism for saints and heroes. It is a piece of everyday advice for sailors or mountaineers. It might be printed in an Alpine guide or a drill book. This paradox is the whole principle of courage; even of quite earthly or quite brutal courage. A man cut off by the sea may save his life if he will risk it on the precipice. He can only get away from death by continually stepping within an inch of it. A soldier surrounded by enemies, if he is to cut his way out, needs to combine a strong desire for living with a strange carelessness about dying. He must not merely cling to life, for then he will be a coward, and will not escape. He must not merely wait for death, for then

I

he will be a suicide, and will not escape. He must seek his life in a spirit of furious indifference to it; he must desire life like water, and yet drink death like wine. No philosopher, I fancy, has ever expressed this romantic riddle with adequate lucidity, and I certainly have not done so. But Christianity has done more: it has marked the limits of it in the awful graves of the suicide and the hero, showing the distance between him who dies for the sake of living and him who dies for the sake of dying. And it has held up ever since above the European lances the banner of the mystery of chivalry: the Christian courage, which is a disdain of death; not the Chinese courage, which is a disdain of life." [1]

The same is true of all the things of the mind, although it has not yet been sufficiently made use of as an educational method. Even brilliant gifts do not of themselves enable a person to win mastery without pain. For instance, the talents of a first-rate musical virtuoso will be of very little service to him, unless he give himself to years of drudgery which it is not worth

[1] G. K. Chesterton, *Orthodoxy* (1909), pp. 168, 169.

the while of the average person to devote to that exercise. The apparent freedom of a violinist is the crown of a long agony of effort. Mere cleverness, used only to save its possessor trouble, leads to nothing but dilettantism, and is the ruin of many brilliant undergraduates. Even freedom in literary composition comes commonly only after vast toil. John Henry Newman is, in many judgments, the writer of the finest English we have; yet he wrote everything three times. It seems to be a law of life that, somehow or other, pain forms an element in everything that is living and joyful. "Power of life," as Hort said once, "means power of suffering." It is true that success comes from our having the spirit of the game in what we do, and that for this end our interest, which is in some way delight, must be invoked; yet how little do we realise that even interest very often does not come at first, and may indeed only arise after much compulsion. "All tastes that are worth having are acquired tastes," is a maxim worth remembering; and that is but a way of saying that those interests which afford us greatest satisfaction were at first discerned only as painful. By the force either of our own will or of some external compulsion, we are driven into doing something, until, like reading a foreign language, it becomes eventually a delight; then, when the spirit of the game is once aroused, whatever the object—money-getting, study, spiritual or bodily development—that very interest carries us through all kinds of difficulties, which, apart from such interest, we should pronounce overwhelming. The spirit of the sportsman who, foreseeing an obstacle, cries " There's a nice hill to run up," is by universal consent the only spirit which makes even our natural life, with its network of difficulties, possible to encounter.

This may all seem obvious; what is not obvious, and is often overlooked, is its congruity with the doctrine of cross-bearing. Indeed it is a part of it. It springs from the truth that man is not merely a being of the moment, but a spirit which endures. If the self were not going on, where would be the use of training of any kind ? If the boy is not ever to become the man, how are we to justify all that training of powers and faculties which h can only use in the future ?

Part of it may indeed be of the nature of gymnastic; and the mere exercise of his powers, mental or bodily, will give a greater zest to life, even at the moment, than would result from an entirely capricious choice of his own pleasure from hour to hour. Still, in some of these forms of gymnastic, it is very much the future that is being thought of; that is, it is justified because he is to grow up. Success in education or adventure or in any form of life comes from the balance between that pain which is a feature of all growth, and that delight which comes from life rejoicing in itself.

Even the mystic tells the same tale. Whatever may be our view of the teaching of the mystics as a whole, there can be no doubt that they give us a vivid present-ment of actual experience. If we read *The Dark Night of the Soul* of St. John of the Cross, or the autobiography of St. Teresa, or the yet more touching one of Suso, is not the same phenomenon apparent? Pain, loss, doubt, gloom,—all must be endured, even embraced, until at last it reaches almost to breaking-point, paralleled only by the dereliction cry. But this is not the end. After this sense of desolation—but only after it—comes the bridal of the soul, that intimate union with God which results in raptures beyond the reach of words, a joy which overcomes and subsumes the pain, and is not to be reached without it.

The need of the final desolation is apparent from another circumstance which in itself is a part of our argument. Love is of such a nature that sacrifice—giving—is its final expression, and itself transmutes the anguish, whether physical or mental, undergone for the beloved, into joy. This is a fact of human, no less than of Divine, love. Consequently, for the sacrifice of the lover of God to be real and complete, it may or may not be needful that he should go through the various forms of either bodily or mental anguish. If he does, all of them are transmuted by the alembic of love—a fact which we can see in the life of any mother. For this sacrifice of the soul, which is the test and reality of love, to be complete, there must inevitably be the sense of desolation, of aloneness; otherwise the soul can never truly possess itself, and all its sacrifice is unreal. That seems to be partly, at least, the ground of our Lord's Passion, and of those experiences so universal among the mystics.

Anyhow, this fact is established. All the most severe, and apparently unwise, ascetic practices of mystics like Suso are ultimately of the joyous type. Their aim is the bridal union of the soul with God. They are dying in order to live; and in this, as in every other case, whether or no we approve of all the means adopted, we cannot deny either that they were effective and the joy sought for was ultimately attained, or, as we have seen, that some form of this agony is essential if the soul is ever to come to its own. In any form of education the difficult point is always the loneliness of spirit in which the crisis, of whatever kind it be, must be passed. This loneliness is a necessary result of the uniqueness of the self; and unless we pass through it we cannot rise to the possession of our own individuality.

So far as I can see, this pain and stress is in some form a necessity for all beings who are developing. They must ever be rising on stepping-stones of their dead selves to

higher things; and this process of dying
and rising again daily and hourly cannot
be accomplished without pain. When St.
Paul said, " I die daily," he was expressing
what, in a less degree and with far less
acute consciousness of it, must take place not
merely in the life of every Christian, but in
that of any man or woman who advances
in spiritual or moral or intellectual or even
bodily accomplishment; only it will depend
on the nature of the advance, and the time
of life, how far this " daily dying " is felt to
involve the whole range of the life or only
parts of it. But it takes place in the life of
the soldier no less than in that of the saint;
it makes up the matter of the experience of
the student no less than of the athlete, and
of the artist along with the day-labourer.
Christianity is not singular in its doctrine
of the need of renunciation, of " dying to
live "; it is not unnatural or inhuman, either
in end or in means. For the end is that of
richer life; and the means, that which is
seen—alike by reflection and by experience
—to be the condition *sine qua non* of all
development. Where the Christian faith
is different is that it leaves no part of us

unaffected by this call to bear the cross, and literally demands that we lose the self to save it; and that it shows all this to be worth while. Some of this discipline would undoubtedly be necessary even if man were mortal; as things are, he could not get the most out of this life, considered as a closed circle, if he were not ready within limits to risk it. But it is the fact that he is making a character for eternity which is the postulate of the Christian faith; and it is through the Risen Life, and that only, that we can justify that long process of discipline by which the soul comes to its home.

Further, as we hinted, all this receives its interpretation only on the Christian view of Reality. Roughly speaking, that is summed up in the doctrine that God is Love. It is because the universe is ultimately spiritual, and love is the law of its being, that renunciation can be seen to hold its place in the total scheme. Even the first beginnings of love, interest in an end far off, will give us power and even delight in the difficulties and suffering which are the conditions of that achievement. Love itself is of so strange and mystic a nature, that, though it begins in delight, it cannot realise itself without pain. It cannot know itself apart from sacrifice. Mere liking, mere pleasure, has not in it that joy of mutual giving in which consists the love between persons; indeed, it is in the difference between a love which gives and a liking which only takes that lies the distinction between love and lust. It does not lie in the presence or absence of the sensuous element. This may be present in a perfect love, and it may be absent in a mere pleasurable liking, which is essentially lustful. Now giving—sacrifice—means in the last resort something that costs. Thus the love of God no less than the love of man leads in the very measure of its reality to the need of sacrifice. We must do something to show our friendship; and, in the last resort, that brings us to the offering of self. As we saw above, that offering cannot be completed by any merely bodily or mental anguish; for, so long as we are assured of the love of the other, that suffering is itself transformed. It must go on till it reaches that sense of loss and loneliness of which the culminating expression was the cry from the Cross.

Thus there are good grounds for our holding that, so far from the Christian ideal of cross-bearing being inhuman, it is congruous—alike in end and means—with the whole method of the development of human life; and that it gives to what otherwise might seem a harsh discipline, forced on us by the awryness of things, its true spiritual interpretation in the love of God for man and of man for God, and that love within the Godhead which reached its earthly symbol in the life of Jesus.

This statement may seem commonplace; but we need it greatly at this moment, when such views are scouted by the doctrine of a self-centred development, which misconceives alike the nature of personality and the meaning of development. The truly perverse and inhuman ethic is that of the voluptuary. If you make immediate satisfaction your end, you subject the individual to the moment, you destroy his powers of growth, and in the long run you make impossible that very fulness of joy which you have preached. Indeed such doctrine is plausible only in so far as it is preached to those who, in some particular, either of body or mind, have gone through a discipline which is its contradiction, and have acquired through long drudgery and effort a delight in some form of human activity which seems like second nature. Even the decadent æsthete has not reached his little kingdom of taste without many tears by the way, and has probably cried over his books before he could read. Herbert Spencer defined education as the power to do what you ought when you ought, whether you like it or not. Lately, however, we have been told of a new system, in which the sole motive is to be interest; children are never to be checked. It may be workable under the headship of one with a genius for managing children; but, if applied by the average person, it would merely produce the normal results of spoiling. Surely with the general contempt of all notion of discipline, there is a danger that the world of civilised mankind may become a world of spoiled children. The presupposition which underlies much popular fiction is just this: anything you passionately want to do, you ought to do, and there must be something wrong in any ethical code which forbids you to do it. Individualism rampant, with discipline scouted, has been the ideal of many since Rabelais imagined the Abbey of Theleme. In the name of personality there is asserted a freedom which is the very denial of personality; for personality can come to itself only in society, and that involves a measure of order and continuity. But these new ideals tend to allow the supremacy of the moment, and to make of man a mere bubble on the stream. All of us know the struggle between wishes and will—between what we like at the moment and what we want to be; and there is much in our most popular writing which tends to tilt the balance all on the side of momentary desire.

It is curious that some of those who are acclaimed as prophets of this tendency preached a very different ideal from what their *soi-disant* disciples imagine. No one will accuse Nietzsche of any liking for Christian morals; yet he was far enough from preaching the supremacy of the moment. Self-control of an austere quality must go to the making of the superman, who is represented more closely by the highly trained Spartan aristocrat than by any modern voluptuary. His notion of a new race—a conquering group—includes essentially the ideals of a proud obedience, and a "long will" which will sacrifice any pleasure of the moment to the end it has in view. One page in his writings describes the advantage of a hard discipline in terms which could not be equalled in the severest ideals of Christian education: "*The type of my disciples.*—To such men as *concern me in any way* I wish suffering, desolation, sickness, ill-treatment, indignities of all kinds. I wish them to be acquainted with profound self-contempt, with the martyrdom of self-distrust, with the misery of the defeated : I have no pity for them ; because I wish them to have the only thing which to-day proves whether a man has any value or not, namely, *the capacity of sticking to his guns.*" [1] And again : "I cannot see how anyone can make up for having missed going to *a good school* at the proper time. Such a person does not know himself ; he walks through life without ever having learned to walk. His soft muscles betray themselves at every step. Occasionally life

[1] Nietzsche, *The Will to Power*, Aph. 910. (From the authorised English translation, by permission of Mr. T. N. Foulis, of Edinburgh.)

itself is merciful enough to make a man recover this lost and severe schooling; by means of periods of sickness, perhaps, which exact the utmost will-power and self-control; or by means of a sudden state of poverty, which threatens his wife and child, and which may force a man to such activity as will restore energy to his slackened tendons, and a *tough spirit* to his will to live. The most desirable thing of all, however, is under all circumstances to have severe discipline *at the right time*, i.e. at that age when it makes us proud that people should expect great things from us. For this is what distinguishes hard schooling, as good schooling, from every other schooling, namely, that a good deal is demanded, that a good deal is severely exacted; that goodness, nay, even excellence itself, is required as if it were normal; that praise is scanty, that leniency is non-existent; that blame is sharp, practical, and without reprieve, and has no regard to talent and antecedents. We are in every way in need of such a school; and this holds good of corporeal as well as of spiritual things; it would be fatal to draw distinctions here!

The same discipline makes the soldier and the scholar efficient; and, looked at more closely, there is no true scholar who has not the instincts of a true soldier in his veins."[1]

Such a notion is a necessity to anyone with a programme; for no programme for humanity but must demand severe self-sacrifice if it is ever to be carried out. In other words, those who have seemed most opposed to the Christian doctrine of self-denial are driven in practice to recommend very similar methods, the moment they attempt to direct the ideals of mankind to any far goal.

We shall, however, do well to remember that not merely Christian morals, but all sense of social discipline is being overruled by the eager self-will of our day and the passion for material enjoyment among the wealthier classes. The desire to escape from the past and to live only in the moment is very imperious, and, with the decay of the sanctions of Puritanism, has become widespread. Poets do but express what is a very prevalent desire in lines such as these of Mr. Sturge-Moore:

[1] Nietzsche, *The Will to Power*, Aph. 912. (From the authorised English translation, by permission of Mr. T. N. Foulis, of Edinburgh.)

" Of men the least bound is the roving seaman
Who hires himself to merchantman or pirate
For single voyages, stays where he may please,
Lives his purse empty in a dozen ports,
And ne'er obeys the ghost of what once was !
His laugh chimes readily; his kiss, no symbol
Of aught to come, but cordial, eager, hot,
Leaves his to-morrow free. With him for com-
    rade
Each day shall be enough, and what is good
Enjoyed, and what is evil borne or cursed.
I go, because I will not have a home,
Or here prefer to there, or near to far.
I go, because I will not have a friend
Lay claim upon my leisure this day week.
I will be melted by each smile that takes me ;
What though a hundred lips should meet with mine!
A vagabond I shall be, as the moon is.
The sun, the waves, the winds, all birds, all beasts,
Are ever on the move, and take what comes ;
They are not parasites like plants and men,
Rooted in that which fed them yesterday.
Not even Memory shall follow Delphis,
For I will yield to all impulse save hers,
Therein alone subject to prescient rigour ;
Lest she should lure me back among the dying—
Pilfer the present for the beggar past.
Free minds must bargain with each greedy
    moment
And seize the most that lies to hand at once." [1]

---

[1] T. Sturge-Moore, *A Sicilian Idyll.* (Duckworth & Co.)

K

These lines are evidence of the spirit which is at work, a spirit which mocks at every ancient sanctity, and (if allowed its unchecked course) would destroy not merely religion, but every institution of social life. It is owing to this attack that it is true to say that "the future of our threatened State lies with the Church."[1]   When we have realised what I have been saying to-day, that the Christian ideal of cross-bearing is at the bottom of all human life that is worthy, we shall be less apt to be dismayed by the many violences that we see around us.   For in the long run the *anima naturaliter humana* must assert itself; and along with the return of the human ideal will eventually come the conviction of many, that the human points on to the Christian, and that Christian ethics are not a system of clericalist taboos, but form the only enduring basis of a noble social life.

[1] Bussell, *Christian Theology and Social Progress*, p. 145.

V

THE DEMOCRACY OF THE CATHOLIC CHURCH

"There is neither Greek nor Jew, circumcision nor un-
circumcision, Barbarian, Scythian, bond nor free; but Christ
is all, and in all." (Col. iii. 11.)

IN these words St. Paul sets forth the truth
that the Christian Church is the spiritual
democracy of mankind. In the Catholic
Church, entered by baptism, living by faith
in a historic Person, and nourished by the
Eucharist, united by a common worship,
and bound by the one universal tie of love,
there are no barriers of sex or race or age or
circumstance. True, there are distinctions
of function; everybody cannot do everything. As St. Paul, himself a stickler for
order in the Church, declares in another
place:

"There are diversities of gifts, but the
"same Spirit. . . . And God hath set some
"in the church, first apostles, secondarily pro-

" phets, thirdly teachers, after that miracles,
" then gifts of healings, helps, governments,
" diversities of tongues. Are all apostles?
" Are all prophets? Are all teachers?
" Are all workers of miracles? Have all
" the gifts of healing? Do all speak with
" tongues? Do all interpret? But covet
" earnestly the best gifts: and yet show I
" unto you a more excellent way." (1 Cor.
xii. 4, 28–31.)

The universality of the appeal of the
Gospel is no ground, as some would affirm,
for denying the need of offices and distinctions within the body. No more is the universality of the gift of the Holy Spirit a
ground for denying the variety of men's
capacity for devotion. These distinctions,
displayed on the one hand in the orders of
the hierarchy, and, on the other, in the special
attribution of the term " saint " to certain
highly endowed souls, are the natural outcome of the rich variety of human life. In no
way do they militate against the fundamental
unity of all members of the Christian Church
or against its Catholic appeal. Only that
" pert and provincial spirit " which Tyrrell
deplored can deem itself affronted by these

inevitable distinctions.   Nothing, indeed, but personal conceit can refuse the title of " saint " to such an one as the Apostle of the Gentiles, or the author of the *Confessions*, or the little poor man of Assisi.

For all that, it remains true that the Catholic Church is a religious democracy in the one sense in which the phrase has a value.   It is a life for all, and not for some. No barrier but his own choice excludes any man.   Its highest act of worship and of communion, the Eucharist, is shared by all ; and the gift is the same to saint and sinner, to priest and layman, to an archbishop and to an artisan.   Entrance into the Church again is free to all and is no matter of tempera-ment or mood.   Rooted in a historic faith, the Church throws her doors open to the wide world.   So long indeed as human sin endures, there will be some who will choose not to enter, but there are none who may not ; and no faculty is needed beyond that of normal humanity.

Modern unbelievers, and some, too, among believers, in a spirit of genial tolerance have been a little too ready to take a different line.   The tendency of much existing talk

is to treat religion as a matter of temperament. Some will say that this peculiar
temperament is denied to them, envying
perhaps those who have it. Viewed in this
way, the religious sense is like artistic or literary gifts—the treasure of the few. To those
who have it not, the doors of the Church
must be eternally barred. We are, then, after
all, Calvinists of a new variety. Even apologists have sometimes taken a similar line,
—arguing, or appearing to argue, as though
only persons who possessed some peculiar
gift were fit critics of the utterances of the
religious consciousness. This line of apologetic is justified, in so far as it means denial
of any logical demonstration of the God of
religion. Nothing seems to me clearer, on
a mere observation of existing facts, than
the certainty that in all these matters the
decisive point is not reached by mere logic—
whether or no the ground be that people can
never be got to agree on the premises.
Supposing, for example, all or some of the
traditional arguments for the being of God
seem to me to be unassailable and I could
rest my faith thereon ; nevertheless I am
bound to admit (as mere fact) that even

among believers many, who know more than
I do, do not think them irrefragable or even
valid; and that many others among instructed people, fully aware of the arguments, have yet rejected all belief in God,
in our sense. But if the arguments were
what they claim to be, disbelief in them
would be possible to no instructed person
outside a lunatic asylum, and we should rank
the unbeliever with a flat-earth fanatic. So
again is it with the historical evidence. No
historical evidence can of itself, and apart
from other considerations, be strong enough
to base a religion upon; for, in order to erect
so mighty a structure as a religion, it must
have to do with facts which in some way or
other are abnormal. The amount of credibility we shall ascribe to the evidence for
anything abnormal will partly depend on
whether or no we believe in the other world,
or at least are willing to accept it as a hypothesis. Apart from this, no existing or
possible historical evidence could ever convince—not even letters written on the sun.
If they believe not Moses and the prophets,
neither will they believe, though one rise
from the dead. And, throughout the world's

history, men of this type always have refused to believe, though One rose from the dead. It was to help the faithful, not to convince the incurably faithless, that our Lord rose that third day.

On these grounds, then, it seems to me true to say that certitude, whether logical or historical, in matters of religion is not to be looked for—*i.e.* that we can have no coercive demonstration which shall force men to believe, whether they will or no. To that extent the apologist is right when he compares the religious sense to artistic or literary tastes, which can find no beauty or even meaning in what to others is the symbol of the glory and the wonder of the world; but such an apologist is wrong if he asserts that there is any man without this sense. Personally, I do not believe that there is any man living without artistic taste; it is less in some than in others, and may be dormant or stifled by other interests; always, however, it is there. In religion, however, the capacity for God-consciousness is, in my judgment, a normal human faculty like any other; all that we know of human life and comparative religion favours the view that it is universal, though often very rudimentary. To make a ground for its denial the existence—under highly artificial conditions — of a certain small number of educated men who either deny it or stifle it, would seem to me no more rational than to deny that man had the capacity to throw stones with his arm because some persons of sedentary life may have lost the power to exercise it. The religious sense is something other than intellectual knowledge, but it is not for that reason less universal; in many ways it is more so.

To take another point. Just at this moment mystical experience is much in vogue. Books on the mystics appear almost weekly. With some this may lead to a denial of true religion to those who have not the gifts or training for these high raptures. It is obvious that the search for so relatively rare a phenomenon may lead to a purely aristocratic conception of religion, or at least to the belief that only the mystic has true religion, and that everyone else gets theirs at second-hand. The Catholic doctrine, however, while it provides a place

for mysticism, avoids this danger. While
it admits the mystic's claim to direct vision
of God, it would assert that he only has, in
a higher degree, what is common to all
Christians through prayer and communion.
The supreme rapture of a St. Teresa or a
St. John is, to the true Catholic, but the
sublimation of what may occur to the most
commonplace Christian in any prayer. Now,
however, the cult of mysticism is in danger
once more of making religion exclusive—a
coterie hobby! It is not new, and very
little different from the Quaker " doctrine
of the inner light." The newly awakened
interest in religious phenomena, coupled
with the fact that mystical knowledge claims
to be direct and first-hand knowledge, is
causing many people to attach a value to
the deliverance of the mystical consciousness
out of all proportion to every other element
of religious knowledge, and to treat the
mystic as the sole authority. Such a tendency, if unchecked, would deliver us, tied
and bound, into pure subjectivism, and is in
no way compatible with the Christian faith.
The mystic's rapture is not confined to
Christians ; there seems no reason to doubt

that it was experienced by Plotinus.   Apart from some outside criterion, every mystic may tell us different things ; and we shall, literally, not know where we are.   Hermann is, I think, not justified in his attempt to set Christianity on the one side, and mysticism on the other, as two opposing religions ; [1] but there is danger in a mysticism not subject to the criteria of faith in the historic reality of Christ and His Church.   Despite the common opinion of this country, I believe that Bossuet discerned the dangerous tendency of a fashion for mysticism, and that the system of Fénelon was essentially aristocratic—aristocratic in the religious sense— a religion for the spiritually gifted.   The limits, and also the value, of mysticism have recently been well examined in two admirable essays in the *Journal of Theological Studies* by the Rev. Oliver Quick.[2]

Historically, mysticism has often tended to fade into Pantheism, always the enduring enemy of Christianity with its insistence on the worth of the individual and the distinct-

[1] Hermann, *The Communion of the Christian with God.*

[2] *i.e.* January and October, 1912.   But I think Mr. Quick goes too far in the same direction as Hermann.

ness of God. Practically it is bound to
make the real *terrain* of religion the play-
ground of a few specially endowed persons,
with the great mass of men and women
either outside the pale or subsisting on the
crumbs that fall from the rich man's table.
In the religious community it would concentrate power in the hands of an absolute
oligarchy of *illuminati*, which would be far
more dangerous to the liberty of the common
man than the most authoritative hierarchy
ever known. Yet just now mysticism seems
to be thought by many to be the last word
of religious freedom ; while the Church, with
her welcome for all, is treated as enslaving
and conventional.

Calvinism has to meet a similar attack.
Few, I suppose, to-day would share the
Calvinist doctrine that God has created the
world in order that, through Adam's sin
predestined, the masses of men might suffer
eternal torture, thereby to increase the bliss
of the elect. Its injustice is what strikes
us most. What I wish, however, here to
notice is its purely oligarchic character.
Historically Puritanism always was oligarchic ; history has never suffered a deeper

perversion than in the popular notion that
Puritans were democrats.   Calvin certainly
never professed to be one.   The root-idea
of Calvinism is the faith that Christ did
not die for all, and that Christianity is a
coterie of religious aristocrats; and even in
the last century M'Cleod Campbell was
condemned for asserting the contrary.

Oligarchy in religion takes many forms;
but in one way or another it is at the
bottom of nearly all the Protestant systems.
Luther went through a devastating experience, and came finally to something
real.   This he tried to universalise into his
doctrine of justification by faith.   From the
days of Luther it has been the aim of every
" believer "—in the Protestant sense—to go
through an experience at least analogous.
Those who have it not, and are without
this feeling of assurance, are not to be
treated as true Christians.   All forms of
Christian teaching which lay very great
stress on conversion are guilty of this error.
They try to universalise a religious phenomenon which, though not rare, is not, and is
never intended to be, the experience of all
Christians.   They tend to deny the title of

Christian to the baptized and confirmed Churchman of phlegmatic temper, who just goes straight on. They make a particular form of temperament the norm for every man, and condemn many true servants of Christ to a place outside the pale. Although they may declaim against sacerdotalism as setting up barriers between man and God, they themselves set up a worse barrier; for they make God's "grace" conditional on a peculiar feeling, and, if they could, would confine the Church to persons of one kind of temperament. Incidentally they must deny all real place in the Church to children, at any rate until they are old enough to experience, or try to experience, this nerve-storm. In a book by a well-known literary man, which outweighs in value all his other contributions, Mr. Gosse's *Father and Son*, we can see something of the ravages wrought by this unnatural system. In his case it was connected with a very narrow form of creed—"Plymouth Brethrenism"; but the phenomenon is not confined to these doctrines. What we condemn is the attempt to make the child at about ten years old go through all the spiritual agonies which accompany the conversion of the "notorious evil liver," and the effort to treat him as an adult. Puritanism, although in its inculcation of an austere sense of duty it has added much to the moral fibre of the race, has yet never found any adequate place for the child in the Church. For in its creed it is not baptism, but conversion, that marks the entrance; and the child is outside until he copies the experience of the adult. Thus, in its exclusion (*a*) of children, (*b*) of all who do not go through a special form of conversion—which, in one view, should even be definitely dated—the doctrine of conversion, if preached exclusively, means a denial of the universality of the Gospel.

How different is the method of the Catholic Church! The membership begins with baptism, and is thus treated as independent of feeling and temperament. With its conception of the Christian life as a growth, nourished by the sacraments, it can find a place for the child and for every kind of character, while in no way denying the need, in the case of some, for those cataclysms of the spirit that are called conversion. For we are not to jump from one extreme to the other. To deny the need of the preaching of conversion is just as much to narrow the Gospel as to over-emphasise it is. The Church, if it uses not merely the sacrament of the Lord's Body and Blood, but also the methods of penitence and the power of absolution, has a means of recalling every wanderer and of assuring the most hardened sinner of this hope. Many men and women, nourished in the comfortable purlieus of Anglican decorum, when they find themselves faced either with their earlier life or with some deep fall, are without the knowledge how to obtain pardon. Deeming the Church the home of respectable people, they feel she is not for them, and forego altogether the practice of religion; but for such (and there are many) the preaching of evangelical conversion and the value of confession is the one hope. But it all needs to be done within the circle of the whole; and the fact must be allowed for, that what is good for one type is not needed for another.

We are not, as some would have it, to deny the value of emotion in religion.

Emotion is no less a gift of God than intellect or character; and without it we should have no art. To condemn emotion in a religion whose idea is love is to talk nonsense. All I am arguing is that emotion in religion needs very careful direction, or it may drop us from spiritual heights to moral depths; and that, even apart from that danger, those persons who are full of religious emotion are not to judge as beneath them others who have little; and that, above all things, we must seek to free ourselves from the notion that religion is a matter of sentiment. No danger of greater import besets the Church at the moment than that by which the clergy, instead of being a body of priests bearing the Cross of Christ, may become a mere set of gentlemen "interested in religion"; and the laity, on their part, may come to consist of those circles of men and women who have felt a special kind of thrill. The evil is confined to no one party. It may be found, as I have said, among people who are never so happy as when they are singing "Safe in the arms of Jesus," condemning all who are not; and it may be found no less among those who are learned in the

L

colours of the festivals, and utter the word
" Catholic " with an unction which would
give pause to the rhetoric of a Rev. Mr.
Stiggins. The word " Catholic " is employed
by a certain set of party men with a very
similar connotation to that of " Christian,"
as used by some of the pietist school; in
both cases a narrowness of interpretation
is given which is at variance with the real
democracy of the Church. In each case
the error is the same; religion is identified
with a certain interest or pleasure; and those
who cannot have this are treated as without
religion.

Opposed to this insistence on a kind of
experience of which only some men are
capable, we have in the revelation of Jesus
Christ a doctrine which is universal. All its
theology is rooted in a life and brought back
thereto; and it is thereby saved from becoming a mere intellectual system. Embodied
in a historic person, its object of worship is
as familiar as our own brother, as mysterious as every child. Nothing esoteric, or only
for the few, hangs about the Gospel; all
may share it who will. The same contrast
appears in the matter of practice. The

Protestant Evangelical spirit (where it remains Christian—I am not speaking here of its drop into mere Unitarianism) has never yet escaped the danger that besets all systems which lay stress on feeling. Now at last it has come about that to many people, both believers and others, religion is merely a special form of emotion. All principles, creeds, ethics are being thrown aside; and we are told it will be all right if we feel right.

Many people will gravely affirm that in such matters as prayer, worship, charity, no principle is concerned, and that our one guide is our own mind. Common sense, indeed, makes short work of such suggestions. In no other part of a normal life would we trust ourselves without reserve to caprice; in religion, however, good sense is the last thing needed. So much has it become a matter of feeling that sentimentalism is really believed by many to be a principle. The same tendency has entered theology. All the more austere elements are slurred. It is not nice to think of pain. Many people dislike the crucifix; and in some cases I am persuaded that the ground of this dislike is the fact that it is a representation of suffering. This is repulsive to the present-day laxity which idolises mere good-nature, and thinks of God's love as the feeling of a foolish mother for her spoilt children. Other ages may have over-emphasised the meaning of judgment, and interpreted crudely certain words of Christ. Yet there can be small doubt that, if religion is concerned with reality, it must needs have an austere side. Only a superficial reading of the Gospel can fail to see this. A theology which is universal cannot ignore pain and sin, or the element of retribution in the punishments of a living God. "There is nothing so merciless as the mercy of God" is a saying which reflects far more of the character of reality than do the sentimental maunderings of fashionable religion. The more intense love is, even as we know it, the less will it shrink from causing pain to the beloved, if an adequate object is to be gained by inflicting it.

Once more. The Christian Gospel makes an appeal which is universal because it starts from the bottom. Its God is One Who died as a criminal, and the Cross is its

throne.   True, it involves a philosophy of life
and a system of ethics, but it is more than
either of these; it is life itself.   All the
systems which try to turn it into the one
or the other and no more, have in them this
fatal flaw;—they are abstract and partial.
They appeal only to one sort of man or to one
part of his being.   They are aristocratic at
bottom, supercilious of the common man.
People often ask why God did not become
Incarnate in a thinker or a philosopher; but
in that case He would have been claimed by
them as "one of us," and would have worn
His rank to all eternity; and the common
man or woman would never have found
in Him a friend.   There would be no poor
people kneeling before the crucifix; nor
could a child have sung the hymns it loves.
Such words as these would not have been
written:

> "Little Jesus, wast Thou shy
>   Once, and just so small as I?
> And what did it feel like to be
> Out of Heaven, and just like me?
> Did'st Thou sometimes think of *there*,
> And ask where all the angels were?
> I should think that I would cry
> For my house all made of sky;

I would look about the air,
And wonder where my angels were;
And at waking 'twould distress me—
Not an angel there to dress me!
Had'st Thou ever any toys,
Like us little girls and boys?
And did'st Thou play in Heaven with all
The angels that were not too tall,
With stars for marbles?   Did the things
Play *Can you see me?* through their wings?
And did Thy Mother let Thee spoil
Thy robes, with playing on *our* soil?
How nice to have them always new
In Heaven, because 'twas quite clean blue!

Did'st Thou kneel at night to pray,
And did'st Thou join Thy hands, this way?
And did they tire sometimes, being young,
And make the prayer seem very long?
And dost Thou like it best, that we
Should join our hands to pray to Thee?
I used to think, before I knew,
The prayer not said unless we do.
And did Thy Mother at the night
Kiss Thee, and fold the clothes in right?
And did'st Thou feel quite good in bed,
Kissed, and sweet, and Thy prayers said?

Thou can'st not have forgotten all
That it feels like to be small:
And Thou know'st I cannot pray
To Thee in my father's way—

When Thou wast so little, say,
Could'st Thou talk Thy Father's way ?—
So, a little Child, come down
And hear a child's tongue like Thy own ;
Take me by the hand and walk,
And listen to my baby-talk.
To Thy Father show my prayer
(He will look, Thou art so fair),
And say : ' O Father, I Thy Son,
Bring the prayer of a little one.'

And He will smile, that children's tongue
Has not changed since Thou wast young." [1]

The Gospel is as universal as life, and no
less mysterious. The worst criminal can
find his Saviour in the Cross ; and the most
highly educated man or woman has not
exhausted the meaning of the words, " I
am the Way, the Truth, and the Life."
Teaching children in the country taught me
much : I learnt then how impossible it is to
identify Christianity with a mere philosophic
idealism ; and the facts of the Gospel and
its dogmas (provided simple words are used)
are quite natural to the young. Dogma,
it is said, should not be taught to children ;
but it would be truer to say that it is the

[1] Francis Thompson, *New Poems*, pp. 151–153. (Burns & Oates.)

only thing you can teach them. After all, however much the intellectualist may pour scorn on others, intellectualism is always oligarchic : and our Lord did say, " I thank Thee, O Father, ... that Thou hast hid these things from the wise and prudent, and hast revealed them unto babes," [1] and He must have meant something by His words. What was a condition of the original Gospel will not hinder its continuance ; and it is only our lack of faith that thinks otherwise.

Perhaps, however, it is in the matter of worship that the universal character of the Catholic religion is most strikingly vindicated. Protestants have always depreciated the sacraments ; and, in its developed form, the idea of sacramental grace is scouted as blasphemous superstition. Preaching has ever been the mainstay of Protestantism. There is, by an English Nonconformist divine, no longer with us, a volume on the philosophy of the Christian religion, of great weight and learning.[2] No one would say that the author was not aware of what is said on all sides. Dr. Fairbairn herein lays down that, strictly

[1] St. Matt. xi. 25.
[2] Fairbairn, *The Philosophy of the Christian Religion.*

speaking, the Eucharist is not an act of worship, and declares that preaching is the only true form of it. Here, then, we have the definite avowal of what has often been argued against Puritanism; and with this avowal comes the disclosure of its aristocratic character. Preaching is a matter of gifts, not, like the priesthood, of a conferred function. Anyone may become a priest who fulfils certain conditions; but, through natural incapacity, many will be debarred from offering to God the worship of preaching. Even if we include in the preacher the sympathetic hearer, it would still be true that this notion of worship sets the highest value on mere difference of intellect and temperament. With the sacramental view of religion, on the other hand, the layman comes into his own; and by "layman," here, I mean the person who, φύσει, is a layman, the man with little religious enthusiasm and no leisure. The coster in the East End can enter into the highest act of Christian worship and receive its crowning grace; provided his will be right, it matters no whit whether he feels much or little. All of us know by experience that it is not at

that Communion at which we have felt most
thrilled that we have been helped most on
our journey; very often such help came
when we went with reluctance and endured
with boredom. Our Lord, it has been well
said, was never so deeply united to His
Father as at the moment of the Calvary
cry, because His will was at one with the
Father's, as the Cross showed. It was only
His feeling that was desolate. So it is in
regard to the layman's treasure—the assurance to the man in the street that the gift of
God is not far off, something only accessible
to people of refined taste or highly organised
nervous system, but within the reach of all.

It is universal because it is simple—the
nourishment of life. Rightly for this reason
have the sacraments been called the Exten-
sion of the Incarnation. As God became
manifest in this world of time and space,
incarnate in Christ Jesus, so He limits Himself to material means in the sacrament.
Most of the objections to the sacrament
make valid arguments against the Incarnation; and indeed the latter presents more
difficulties to the imagination. It is easier
to conceive of God communicating Himself

under the veil of the species of bread and wine, than of the long-continued self-limitation involved in His becoming incarnate in growing human life.

Other objections are similar. So far as they spring from inside the Christian Church, they come from a perverted notion of spirit, which makes the material world evil and is, at bottom, Manichean. It is felt to be degrading to God to suppose that pure Spirit can manifest Himself by material means. All this means a denial of the universality of the Gospel and leaves nature to the devil. If God cannot use material means, we must think of the physical universe as in some way existing apart; and we are driven to a conception of God akin to Deism. God is not denied, but He is banished from the world; and all spirituality comes from abstraction. In consequence, religion becomes departmental, the interest of persons of a certain taste, while most of the works of men go on unregarding. This is precisely what has happened during the past three centuries since (to a large extent) the sacramental idea became obscured; the world at large views religion afar off, and all its living interests go on in separation. In the Middle Ages—indeed, to many it is their reproach—art, literature, music, architecture, chivalry, trade guilds, corporate life and government—all were carried on as part of religion. I do not say that the experiment was altogether a success ; but it was a higher ideal of human life than any dominant now.

Lastly, in this matter of the sacraments, it is not irrelevant to point out that the rejection of all this as mere magic leads, in the long run, to the repudiation of miracle ; for it springs from a conception of the physical world which treats it as independent. Hence it is clear that men cannot go on to hold that God makes it the means of His special manifestation, or manipulates the forces of nature in the way we associate with the life of Christ. Certainly it is the fact that in places like Geneva, Germany, Holland, where there has been the most widespread rejection of the sacramental idea, there has been a very general denial of belief, first in miracles, and finally in the Incarnation.

Lastly, sacramental religion is universal in its appeal to a faith in mystery. No error is more widespread among the Sadducees of our day than that of supposing that, to the average man, if he continues to believe in religion, it is a difficulty that neither sacramental grace nor the Incarnation is susceptible of an entirely rationalistic presentment. This is the last thing he wants. Life and logic to him are incommensurable; and he believes no less than Lotze, if on more practical grounds, that "reality is richer than thought." Therefore he will never be deterred by mere logical puzzles from accepting a system which he finds practically helpful. I do not wish to argue this point at length, for I have said something of it in another work; but the mystery of the Sacraments and the Incarnation is not at this moment a source of trouble to any believing temperament. Far more difficult is what seems to him the unwarrantable lucidity, the cut-and-driedness, of scholastic theology; and in this we may sympathise with him. Let us beware of ever presenting the Christian faith with a cold and legal method, as though it were so many propositions of geometry; and let us always be ready to admit the

vast amount of agnosticism that underlies
every statement about the final reality,
and our knowledge that all words used
about God are mere figures. "All things
"that can be thought, or seen, or told, or
"handled, are as nothing in comparison with
"those things that can neither be thought,
"nor seen, nor told, nor handled."[1]

[1] Giles of Assisi, *The Wisdom of the Simple* (translated by Rev.
T. A. Lacey), chap. ii.

VI

THE COMMUNAL BOND, OR AUTHORITY AND ITS LIMITS

"Lo, I am with you always, even unto the end of the world." (St. Matt. xxviii. 20.)

PROBABLY there is no part of the life of the Church that is more generally distrusted to-day than its claim to authority. The very idea of discipline in regard to spiritual things is scouted; and the notion of any social control of opinion is treated as mid-summer madness. Speaking of his dislike of clergymen, a learned legal friend of mine once said to me: "I suppose it is because they represent the principle of authority." It would be curious to know what lawyers represent, if it be not the same principle in a more rigid form; and ultimately law implies, not merely the power, but the conscience, of the nation reaching its personal reality. Yet this notion is widespread; indeed, with that universal desire for a new

and more vivid life of which I spoke earlier,
it tends to increase. I have been told of
a society to which full membership is impossible except to those who agree to repudiate every kind of authority, alike in
morals and religion. Such a pledge shows
a curious lack of humour, for in itself it is
an authority; still, such a phenomenon is
significant.

Tendencies very similar are displayed by
many who would be shocked if they were
to be called anything but good Christians.
On the one hand, that subjectivism of
which we spoke earlier tends to make men
distrustful of rules. Caprice is made the
arbiter of religious duty in the matter of
worship.

Even in morals the same is often suggested; and present controversies are evidence of this. In regard to divorce the
claim is made, not merely outside but
inside the Church, that she is false to the
spirit of Christ if she insists on even a
modicum of self-restraint. The charge is
not that she draws the line at the wrong
place, but that she draws it at all.

A recent writer in the *Edinburgh Review*

declares, with reference to the report of the Divorce Commission:

"Greater difficulty is involved in the "suggestion that the taking advantage of "extended grounds may lead to the refusal "of the Holy Communion. We believe that "if the Church of England as a whole adopts "such a position it will involve itself in "absolute disaster."[1]

Similar attacks are made on all who would insist on any standard in regard to the Holy Communion, or Orders, and so forth. It is not so much the Confirmation test, nor episcopal orders, as the very notion of a limit, that is disliked. The persons who make these demands seem unable to realise facts. If the Church, however loosely compact, be the society of those inspired by the Christian spirit, clearly she must have some limits; else, in a world which contains men and women of any religion and of none, there will be no way of distinguishing such a body from people with whom Christ, so far from being an object of worship, is not even one of reverence. Grounds for this confusion are sought in the claim that

[1] See *Edinburgh Review* for January 1913, p. 20.

M

Christianity is the religion of love; love in this sense is the amiable geniality to which all acts and thoughts are equally good, as being human; and a religion so formed would be a mere sentimental Pantheism. A world impatient of discipline treats as a blot upon the pure spirit of the Gospel every attempt to maintain a standard in the Church. One writer, far from unfavourably disposed, speaks of us moderns to whom "ecclesiastical discipline has ceased to be even an impertinence." In England, too, the fact of establishment lends colour to the claim that every Englishman has a right to use all the offices of the Church, without fulfilling any moral or spiritual obligations whatever. Even more ludicrous is that form of this dislike to definition which is shown in the claim that an official of the Church should be allowed entire freedom of criticism, while still continuing to exercise his office. Fortunately over here, in the case of Mr. Algernon Sidney Crapsey, you had a golden opportunity of refuting this. Clearly, in a free society like the modern nation, criticism is free, like Churchmanship. It should be no less clear that if criticism of any society, whether political or religious, carries any member of it to the point at which he repudiates its foundations, his only course is to leave it.   Yet entire freedom for any and every kind of historical criticism is now claimed for a priest, not merely as a man, but as a priest continuing to exercise his ministry.   If this claim were admitted, a priest would be right in celebrating the Eucharist even after he had become con-vinced, with Professor Drews or Mr. W. B. Smith, that our Lord never existed at all. Obviously the claim to freedom, laid down in this absolute form, cannot stop at those particular occurrences which the disputants reject.   The principle put forward is not that the events are unimportant, but that the exercise of the priesthood ought to be independent of any and every historical conclusion.   In days like these, when there is a school both in Europe and America which denies the reality, not merely of the miracles, but of the whole earthly life of Christ, it is clear that we might have priests who held this view and held merely to some general faith in the Christian ethic.   Some of the more extreme modernists do, if I mistake not, make this claim.

Nor would the tendency stop here. There is no ground for freeing historical criticism which does not apply equally to the ethical and philosophical. Why should not a man continue to hold the emoluments of (say) a deanery, even though he had convinced himself of the justice of Nietzsche's repudiation of Christian ethics, or of Karl Pearson's doctrines of eugenics and the sexual problem? This was done in Italy in the fifteenth century, and among the " abbés philosophes " in France in the eighteenth. Nor again should their freedom be merely ethical. If the retention of office is to be independent of our opinions—and that is the real purport of the claim—there is no reason why one article of the creed should be held more sacred than another. The existence of a God becomes a test and a limit; Professor Harnack would be no less a drag upon freedom than the Pope. On this view, nothing in the principles of Spinoza need deter a man from holding a bishopric; and the Church might see once more repeated the glorious days of Archbishop Talleyrand.

I do not say that these rights are actually
claimed, though I do not say that they are
not; what seems clear is that they are the
direct and inevitable corollary of the claim
that is made, which is this—in a society
devoted to the worship of a historical Person,
belief in Whom must depend on the reality
of certain events, office—and, of course,
membership—is to be independent of any
belief as to whether those events did or did
not take place.   The claim is put forward
in all sincerity.   There is no ground for the
charge of dishonesty; it is not dishonesty,
it is confusion of thought that is the matter.
For if the Christian Church be a society at
all, she must mean something, and not something else.   If she be attached to Jesus of
Nazareth, the belief in certain historical
events must be incumbent on all who belong
to her.   What this claim of freedom denies
is the fact that the Church is a society.

For if we reflect a little, we shall see that
some limits must perforce belong to the
Church, if she be a corporate society, a
community with a permanent end and a
"general will."   Authority, in fact, arises
out of the very nature of society as such, as

was shown long ago by political philosophers. True, men get rid of authority by that doctrine of the invisible Church which became popular at the Reformation period, and is the real meaning of modern undenominationalism; but this doctrine is really the denial of the social nature of Christianity. If there be no Church other than the indiscernible company of those unknown and unknowable persons predestined to final perseverance, then clearly there can be no Christian society here on earth; the bonds between men are purely subjective and inward, and no person or body of persons can, in the name of Christ, claim any authority.

In this view, there might, it is true, still be groups of professing Christians who choose to act together; and, so long as they exist, the group through its organs must exercise authority over its members. The authority is not an essentially Christian authority, for membership of the group is not, on this view, of the essence of the Christian life; it is something superadded, at the good pleasure of the individual member. No individual need join because he is a Christian; while he remains, he must, it is true, obey its rules, but he can leave it whenever he likes, on any pretext, without impairing his Christianity, just as a man can leave a club without affecting his claim to be an Englishman. That, as I understand it, is the Protestant conception of Church life. It is analogous to the joint-stock company, an association formed purely at will, and united by no bonds but those of contract. Needless to say that many of the Protestant sects hold to a far more intimate and social conception of religion. This is, or was, true in a very special degree of Presbyterianism, of the Baptists, and—in its early days—of Independency ; for Independency asserted the separateness of each congregation, not that of the individual. Protestant individualism, as it works out, results in the position stated above ; but for a long while many groups of Protestants retained much of the Catholic conception of the Church, only they differed as to its constitution.

The Catholic notion of authority asserts that the Christian becomes such only by membership of the Christian society, of which the seal is baptism ; just as an Englishman is an Englishman because he is a member of the English nation and a subject of King George. Moreover, it goes on to assert that he cannot, if he would, repudiate its claims upon him. True, he is free to leave it, and no one can compel him to remain; but if he does leave it, he does so at the peril of his Christianity, for schism is a sin. This is the conception which is largely denied to-day, for it involves the detested notion of authority as inherent in the life of the Christian. Many men, deeply devoted to our Lord, regard all such claims as an infringement of natural liberty, the invention of aspiring priests; others, glorying in the name of Churchmen, would yet repudiate with scorn all attempt at discipline.

The notion of a Churchmanship which involves no authority and needs no discipline flourishes among us to-day, partly owing to the long struggle for civil freedom. So evil is the legacy of the days when civil penalties were the meed of religious difference, that now we touch the opposite extreme. Everyone is free to-day, and rightly free (so far as civil law is concerned), to belong to any religious body he chooses,

and to change it every week. This right,
which is a civil one, is confused by many
with a claim to remain in the Church of
Christ while repudiating every standard of
creed and morals which it sets up. Very
little reflection, however, is needed to show
how untenable is this view. Take the maxim
most commonly commended by the opponents of authority—" Christianity means
the following of Christ." So be it; personal
devotion is avowedly the essence of the
Christian life. But does that involve no
authority? Surely the man who worships
"Jesus as Lord" is no longer his own
master. Many people nowadays seem to
have lost all sense of what the word "Lord"
means. They think of it as an honorific
title, but they forget that it implies lordship,
that we are the slaves, the chattels, of Christ.
This phrase seems to mean to many as much,
and as little, as our Lord's words that a
man's life consisteth not in the abundance
of the things that he possesseth; whereas
most Christians live as though the word
"not" had been deleted. If we have once
accepted the lordship of Christ, we must be
willing to obey Him far beyond the limits

of our immediate judgment.   No personal
loyalty has any meaning if it merely implies
that we shall do what in any case commends
itself to us as wise; it must mean that our
faith in the person trusted is so great that
we shall take it for granted he is right, even
when we cannot see it.   Here, then, we have
the idea of authority entering in with our
very first acceptance of the lordship of
Christ.

Further, it is clear that, since Christ Himself is no longer visibly with us, that lordship can come to us only as mediated by
the society which is His body, the earthly
expression of His Spirit; otherwise the
individual is left to his own caprice, and
his acceptance of authority is only one in
name.   True, a special revelation to each
individual might do away with this necessity;
but how are you to test it, if there be no
external criterion ?   Even the revelation to
St. Paul was submitted to the Church, and
accepted by it as authentic.   Systems which
make the individual Christian the exclusive
judge can end only in complete subjectivism.   This was the case with Luther's
notion of the " liberty of the Christian man "

THE COMMUNAL BOND   187

and the open Bible, until the emergence of
Karlstadt and the Zwickau Prophets and
Anabaptism changed the minds of Luther
and Melanchthon, and forced them back
upon the Catholic creeds and the early
general councils.   If Scripture be made the
sole authority, either we have an anarchy of
conflicting interpretations, or else a dead
system, a mere book religion.   There can be
no real authority save that of a living social
spirit.   It is the merit of the Roman
Catholic system, whatever its failures, that
it has remained true to this, even at those
times when most Protestants were enslaved
to the letter and Anglicans served a closed
tradition.   Papal infallibility at least means
that men are not the bond slaves of the
past.

These false conceptions have their origin
in an erroneous idea of the nature and
meaning of authority.   Authority in religion is the spirit of that vast super-indi-
vidual life of the whole society, which
surrounds its living members like an atmosphere, to which all without exception contribute some element, and which sometimes,
though rarely, becomes crystallised in definite

commands and creeds. Authority is the expression of the sociality of man which we
discussed in our second lecture, and saw to
be the natural foundation of the Church.
It arises from the fact that individuals, bound
together in community for permanent ends,
are changed by their union ; that the life
of the community and its members is
spiritual and interpenetrating.

Let us take an instance from a society we
have all been through—school life. What
is the nature of authority in the form of communal existence which we enjoy in a highly
organised school, concerned with the whole
life, not the mere instruction, of its members?
Does it consist in the commands of the
head-master ? I trow not. Is it in his
power, even including that of all his delegates—under-masters and prefects—to issue
commands ? Hardly. Something it is,
deeper and more subtle than any powers of
command. A boy might comply with every
one of these and attain but little of the
school spirit ; he might violate all quite
often, and yet have all its virtue. Surely
the authority of a school, while it includes
all the elements I mentioned above, is

rather to be found in the altogetherness of
the social life of its members, including those
gone from it.   The total pressure of this
on any new boy would come to him as its
authority.   Some of this (a very little) is
written in rules; more of it is crystallised
into public opinion.   More still is indefin-
able—a general spirit, what one calls "tone,"
constantly changing yet always continuous,
so subtle that it may differ very deeply in
two schools of the same date and origin,
recruited from the same classes, serving the
same ends, and organised in precisely similar
fashion and with external characteristics all
but identical.   Much of this authority is
too subtle to be put into words—like the
sub-conscious elements of our individual life.
Let us observe, moreover, that it has one
inalienable note.   All alike share it; all in
some way submit to it; and all contribute
to it.   Not the newest or the least effective
member but makes some difference, either
by his character or by the lack of it; nor, on
the other hand, can the strongest or most
influential person ever act alone.   His effect
on the school, even if every direct order he
gives is obeyed without question, must in

the long run be mediated in a thousand
ways by the number of smaller personalities
without whom he cannot act, and not merely
by the number, or by the school as a whole,
but by the corporate spirit of its parts; the
body of masters, the body of prefects, the
spirit of each house, of each form, of any and
every group that is in any way permanent.
Arnold did not create the Rugby spirit by
his "mere and proper motion," any more
than Arnold himself would have been what
he was but for Winchester. The Rugby
spirit was the synthesis of the personality of
Arnold and of that communal life of which,
though the highest, he was after all only
one member.

On these grounds we can see how this
authority is never a purely external thing.
To the new recruit it seems so; but even
he never wants to be anything but a public-
school boy, and so far gives it his inner
assent. First of all; it presents itself as a
system of strange taboos and hostile individuals. It strikes him as a prison; gradually it becomes a home. Taking part in its
life, he finds that what seemed arbitrary is
so natural that he cannot understand how

any boy could ever want it different. Many
customs which seem hard he learns to value,
for he begins, after a time, to see that his
inner nature demands this hardness. Before
his days at school are half through, his early
troubles have been seen by him to be a
condition of real life ; and he begins to pity
those so placed that they do not have any
fagging or knocking about. " No chasten-
ing for the present seemeth to be joyous, but
grievous ; nevertheless afterward it yieldeth
the peaceable fruit of righteousness unto
them that are exercised thereby." [1] Some of
these truths he sees early ; in other matters he
only realises it later on. Nearly everyone,
however, admits later on in life that the chief
defect of his training has been in the parts
where his caprice was indulged, and authority
did not intervene to help his real mind, at the
expense of his immediate comfort. What I
mean by saying that the discipline is only
partially external, is that not merely does
the discipline show itself as the condition of
freedom, whether in mind or body, but that
his inner mind has always been that of
growing to be a true man ; and that the

[1] Heb. xii. 11.

system of authority expresses this, even
when it contradicts his inclination. Like
one learning to row, he wants to be an oarsman; and he has to learn that every single
movement of his body which seems natural
is wrong, and that he can get freedom only
by relying on the experience of others, *i.e.*
authority. Further, he learns that while
the system seems to press upon and limit
his individuality in many ways as compared,
say, with the freedom of holidays, that is
only appearance; and that only in this social
atmosphere can his personality grow to
realise itself. Perhaps, too, he can compare
what it has made him with some other who
has been without the training; and he finds
that what seemed to destroy his very personality has been the true condition of its
development.

All this may seem trivial. Believe me,
it is not so. Social life in every form has
common elements; and it is well to begin
from what has been vital experience.
Moreover, the nature of authority in the
Church has been so strangely misconceived,
alike by those who support and by those
who reject it, that it seemed worth while

to make it as clear as may be, within the limits of space at my command.

What we need most to realise is that authority in the Church of God is the expression of the life of the whole Christian community, and no single member but bears his part. Of all dangers which beset the statement of the idea of authority, none at this moment is so serious as that which views it purely as external command. The moment that notion is accepted, we are far on the way to the notion that the duty of the majority is merely passive ; as Bishop Horsley said : " The people have nothing to do with the laws except to obey them." With this view first of all the Church begins for practical purposes to consist of the hierarchy, facing the laity as almost a foreign body. The turn of the clergy comes next, and all power is concentrated in the prelates. Finally, the principle works itself out to its extreme, and the Papacy absorbs in itself every kind of jurisdiction and becomes the source of all truth. Pius X might say of himself, " L'église c'est moi," with more truth than the analogous words were ever ascribed to Louis XIV. The

N

Encyclical *Pascendi* which condemned the
Modernists had, in my judgment, fewer
defects than many ascribed to it; but there
was one capital error. The laity were denied
any real right in the Church. Long ago,
in the fourteenth century, a pamphleteer
—probably an Englishman—in the famous
Dialogue between a Knight and Clerk, discerned the dangers that lay in the theory
of Papal autocracy, and declared that, if the
views then fashionable among the canonists
were accepted, the Church would be reduced to slavery. This is precisely what
has happened in the development of ultramontane doctrine to its full expression in
the Vatican decree.

We ought, however, to bear in mind
that this evil lies deeper than the Papal
theory. It comes from a conception of
authority which views it as purely external,
and does not see that it is at once external
and immanent. That is one reason why I
drew the illustration of school life. All
along, the boy is anxious to become a man;
but he shrinks from the various labours of
Hercules, and only by compulsion under-
goes them. By and by he sees that all

that seemed to him most hostile was in reality friendly, and that he must needs go through these things if he would attain the enduring treasure of manliness, whether of body, mind, or character. In the same way the Christian intends to follow Christ, but loves his own will; and only by the pressure of the social power of the Christian body can he be brought to learn what acceptance of Christ involves. This is the gist of St. Paul's first letter to the Corinthians. Yet this pressure, though felt as external, is never so entirely; if it were, we could not even be attracted by the Church. Its authority lies without, but it answers to something within; and, even where our momentary desire would draw back, our will is at one with the command of the society—like an oarsman, worn out with paddling, who would not for worlds defy the bidding of the coach to "row."

Further, although on the one hand the individual is subject to authority, yet his individual uniqueness is ever to be borne in mind. Authority comes to us with a strong presumption. It is always more probable than not that we shall be wrong if we

contradict it; but it is only a presumption.
Our own conscience must in the last resort
decide our action. If, after taking every
means to enlighten it, and having all regard
to that voice which claims to speak with the
accumulated experience of generations of
faithful men, we still find ourselves unable
to think its utterance other than clearly
wrong, then we are bound to follow conscience and set at nought the whole apparent voice of Christendom. Otherwise
we could not justify Athanasius, or indeed the early Christians, or any convert
from the faith of his fathers.

Thus authority is not infallible—unless
indeed we define infallibility as the knowledge that Christ will never permit the
whole of His Church to go so far wrong
that salvation cannot be had therein; but,
in its ordinary sense of the guaranteed
accuracy of formal propositions, I do not see
that we can ascribe it to the Church. The
infallibility (so far as she possesses it) of the
Church is in her life, in the creative evolution which never ceases. While the cere-
monious and critical pronouncements of the
Church organs at momentous epochs are in

all ages to be received with deference, and indeed may come to us with a weight which is only not overwhelming, I can see no ground for supposing that they are infallible in such a way as to deny the living power of the Church in the present and the future, or to deliver us bound to the " dead hand." It is this enslavement of the present to the past which is feared by many just now; nor are their fears altogether without ground— so mistaken is the conception of authority entertained by many, and the confusion of the real weight to be attached to tradition with a certainty which would only too literally be " dead." Strangely enough, Roman Catholics are saved from this error by their belief in the infallibility of the Pope ; whereas too many Anglicans give way to it, owing to their desire to glorify the epoch of the first four general councils.

Primarily, then, it is to Christ that is due the loyalty of the Christian, and through Him to that living society which is inspired by His Spirit ; but it is the living body, not the society as it was some centuries ago, or little pieces broken off from its life. The extreme modernists were, in my judgment, in error when they asserted a spiritual idealism independent of history; and they were far more liable than most of them would admit to the charges of the Papal Encyclical. They carried the notion of the Divine Immanence to the extreme; but on the ethics of conformity they were in the main right, and were nearer to a true conception of authority than their adversaries. Modernist thinkers are justified when they say that loyalty to the formularies of the Church does not mean the assent to an aggregate of isolated statements, each in a pigeon-hole, but rather the submission to that majestic communal life of which creeds are the expression. This of course is not to deny that creeds may be analysed or argued over, piece by piece. It bears its analogy to what I said in the first lecture on our attitude to the historical problem. There we saw that the real problem is as to the total character of the experience—whether or no we can call it supernatural. That, however, does not preclude the analytical and critical study of the separate items in the Gospel narrative; it merely puts such study in its proper place. So with faith and the creeds. We may discuss each point separately; but what is laid upon the individual to determine is whether the voice which speaks in the Church is the voice of God. If he believes that, it is not merely his right but his duty, since every statement about God is figurative, to make use of that symbolism which has come to express it. Englishmen do not enough remember that the proper title of a creed is "symbol."

Such loyalty on general grounds is all that is really possible, in the case of a society with so long and complex a history as the Church of Christ. The ethics of conformity is not an easy topic; and everybody is apt to level charges of insincerity at those who omit some one element which to them is crucial. It may be so, yet in all good faith the others may not believe that; and loyalty is possible only to the society as a whole. Newman, who here as elsewhere showed his amazing insight into the psychology of belief, laid down in Tract XC the principles without which no man of any party can justify his allegiance. Certainly, dishonesty cannot be charged against a man who lays his cards on the table, whether his

views are those of Zwinglian, Papist, or
Liberal. The spirit of a nation or a church
is a thing neither of to-day nor of yesterday;
and no man is necessarily out of harmony
with it because he does not approve of the
government of the day. Tory denouncers
of Lloyd George do not cease to be Englishmen. Some modernist Roman not cate-
gorically condemned, if he feels himself at
one with the spirit of the Church, is justified
in his continuance, even though to many
others his position appears untenable, and
they would not hold it themselves. Doubtless to deny something that is officially
declared to be essential and to conceal that
denial is very like hypocrisy, certainly in a
minister; but of this I am not thinking.
Charges of disloyalty arise commonly out
of not the concealment but the outspoken-
ness of the victim—as for instance in the
case of " Ideal Ward." Doubtless he was
wrong; but he was not dishonest.

For the rest, neither Englishman nor
Roman Catholic ought ever to confuse the
Church with her officials. It is a capital
error to take the " curia " for the state. The
true source and meaning of authority in the

Church is the pressure upon the individual
of the human-divine life of the great society,
which bears in every act the tears of the
saints and the ardours of the martyrs and
lives yet by the Pentecostal breath. No
one will maintain a right attitude who
makes himself the measure of all things, and
treats with a supercilious criticism the movement of this mighty life, living with the
prayers of all the ages and joyous with the
smile of the redeemed. Belief in the utter
independence of the individual is the root of
all error, alike in politics and in religion.
On the other hand, authority will drop into
tyranny if it fails to allow for the real uniqueness of the individual life, and of the
smaller societies within the whole. That
notion of authority which reaches its limit
in Ultramontanism is, at bottom, a false
legalism, accepted from the antique city
state, to which the individual was only a
means, developed in the jurists' theory of
the Roman Law, and transferred during the
course of the Middle Ages from the civil
power to the ecclesiastical. This spirit,
however, is not confined to Rome. We
may find it glowing and resplendent in the

breast of some Low Church rector, who,
strong in the parson's freehold, governs his
parish like a drill-sergeant. It was once exercised with entire severity by the Presbyterian
clergy, and still animates the breast of Mr.
Kensit. It is not wholly false ; it expresses
the truth that Christ's rule is a lordship that
comes from above, and that to individual
feeling it must perforce in many cases present itself under the guise of external command. But it ignores the fact that this
command expresses the inner mind of the
Christian *qua* Christian. Ultimately, like
Nebuchadnezzar, it arrays omnipotence on
the one hand and the rightless man of all
" peoples, nations, and languages " on the
other, bowing down before the golden image
of the autocrat. I do not believe that there is
in the universe an authority rigidly absolute,
in the sense of the ultramontane legalist;
God Himself does not command us, indepen-
dently of reason and conscience. The truth
rather sees the spirit of Christ, the authority,
in the Christian body as a whole, and does
not concentrate it in a centre, not even in a
general council. In every organic part of it
there is the Church; *ubi tres ibi ecclesia;* each

nation, patriarchate, diocese, parish, finally the individual Christian, all bear their part, all have an inalienable share in the authority of the Christian life. Finally, all those conceptions of authority which deny to the individual conscience its unique right are shattered on the rock of reality; ultimately, if admitted, they destroy moral responsibility at its root. No less fatal is any conception of the individual Christian which allows him to deal lightly with the past, or to treat with contempt the religious experience of the world and the fundamentally communal character of Christianity. Let us beware of that root of bitterness which springs up through vanity or from that spirit of personal self-assertion which, like Esau, for one morsel of meat, one little piece of caprice, will sell the birthright of our Churchmanship. "For ye know how that afterward, when he would have inherited the blessing, he was rejected; for he found no place of repentance, though he sought it carefully with tears. For ye are not come unto the mount that might be touched, and that burned with fire, nor unto blackness and darkness and tempest, and the sound of a trumpet, and

the voice of words; . . . but ye are come
unto Mount Sion, and unto the city of the
living God, the heavenly Jerusalem, and to
an innumerable company of angels, to the
general assembly and church of the first-
born . . . and to God the Judge of all, and
to the spirits of just men made perfect, and to
Jesus, the Mediator of the new covenant,
and to the blood of sprinkling, that speaketh
better things than that of Abel. See that
ye refuse not Him that speaketh." [1]

NOTE

This chapter owes much to George Tyrrell
and to other writers; Moëhler's *Symbolik*
remains one of the best pieces of apologetic
for sacramental and authoritative religion.
A work by a Scotch divine (Rev. J. H.
Leckie) is very valuable. I quote one or
two passages :

" It is the power of having this experience
which separates him (the prophet) from
common men. His peculiar glory is not
that he can reason, can suffer, can speak ;
it is that he has *seen*. . . . If this be the

[1] Heb. xii. 17–25.

peculiar gift of the prophet, it follows that
his authority depends on it and on nothing
else. His proper power is confined to the
sphere of the talent that has been given
him; it does not in its fulness extend to
other realms of thought and life. When he
is declaring the religious truth which first
also he received he is a master and king,
and compels the assent of men—'He lords
it o'er us with looks of beauty and words
of good.' But his authority is less when
he speaks, not as the seer but as the logician,
when he appears no longer as the preacher
of a faith but as the expounder of a
theology."

"There is, in short, a spiritual atmosphere,
a compelling medium, which surrounds every
revelation, on which every revelation must
depend for the means of reaching the individual heart and soul. This atmosphere
and medium is the product of long ages; it
is the resultant of many varying forces; it
comes of thoughts that have been tested
and tried over and over again, of experiences repeated in different lives, of customs
slowly gathering force 'from precedent to
precedent,' of conventions established by

education and habit, ' of old unhappy far-off things,' and the dear traditions of the Fathers. This element in religious life and history is a thing of incalculable moment; one that, no doubt, contains matters of varying value, and that is liable to be despised by the theorist and reformer, but one also that, for good or for evil, largely determines the thoughts of us all."

" Must you assert of a power that it is incapable of mistake, before you can say that it is worthy of obedience? Is it a condition of trust, in matters of faith, that the object of confidence should be theoretically viewed as raised above the possibility of error ? Must every authority dwell in a place wherein there is light and no darkness at all ?

" In seeking an answer to this question, it is well to remember that, beyond the religious sphere at least, men do not as a rule assert inerrancy of those powers and teachers to whom they yield submission. The right of every government is recognised by its loyal subjects, but they do not dream of saying that it is incapable of mistake."

" The ' Holy Catholic Church,' the Society

of Believers, is the great incarnation of the democratic power in religion. We cannot, indeed, assert that the Church is *only* the embodiment of the democratic authority, for it is the steward of Revelation and exists by the will, and through the indwelling spirit, of its Lord; neither can we say that it contains within itself the *whole* of the believing element in Christendom, since there are many devout persons who do not live in its communion. But we can say with assurance that its *peculiar* weight lies in its expression of the general faith and thought of average Christian people, and we may confidently claim that it is in every age the great organ and interpreter, within Christendom, of the common religious life."

"It is difficult to see how any thinker who believes in Revelation can refuse to attribute authority to that Society which exists as a witness to Revelation. Surely it is clear that the very same reasoning which establishes the authority of God in the soul establishes still more the authority of God in the great spiritual fellowship of those to whom He speaks. It is not possible for

the individual Christian to assert his own
claims to be a witness to things unseen, and
yet refuse profound deference to the testi-
mony of the multitude of his spiritual peers.
If there is life in the twig, much more is
there life in the tree to which it belongs."

"The theoretic authority of the Church
rests not merely on the weight of its teaching, but also on the insufficiency of individualism as an account of the religious life.
To say that the organ of the spiritual
authority is, in an exclusive way, the *individual* soul in communion with God, would
be to ignore the plain facts of experience
and thought.   There is no such thing as
an 'individual' spirit in the absolute sense.
Every self-conscious being is the sharer in a
universal life. He does, indeed, possess something that separates him from his fellows and
constitutes the core of his personality ; but
he has also much which he holds in communion only with all who think and love.
The common life of humanity is not only
an atmosphere that surrounds him : it is an
element that interpenetrates his being—it
is the 'stuff' that he is 'made on.' Take
away from him all that is not peculiar to

himself and proper to his own individuality, and you leave him poor indeed."

"When we consider how little of the entire sum of our inward possessions can be called the fruit of our own communion with the Highest, when we seek to imagine what our state would be apart from the ancient heritage of faith, and apart from the religious Society which is our home, we understand the measure of our subjection to the appointed authorities of the spiritual Order. Of all forms of arrogance there is none that appears to us so futile as the arrogance of a self-dependent piety.

"But in thus acknowledging our reasonable subjection to 'outward' authorities we are conscious of no humiliation, nor of any unfaithfulness to the inner Witness. For we know that these authorities could have no power over us at all were they not of the same nature as the Oracle that speaks within the soul. The light that shines into our hearts we recognise to be the same that has always dimly burned within. The power of the Church is the kindly power of home and our own people; the prophets speak the language that is spoken by all

o

the voices of the spirit; and Jesus, being our Master and Lord, is yet the Son of His Father and our Father, His God and our God.

"The assertion, then, that communion with God is a possibility, and even in some degree an actuality, for all men, does not involve the rejection, but rather the acceptance, of those authorities which we call 'outward' and 'objective.' For, *the acknowledgment of any power in its poorer and narrower forms, involves the fuller acknowledgment of it in those manifestations which are greater and richer.* How shall we attribute weight to the limited experience of the individual religious mind and not far more yield homage to the long and wide and varied experience of the common religious mind, as expressed in the Church?"[1]

In chapter iv., on Authority and Infallibility, the writer makes the distinction between the two quite clear.

[1] See Rev. J. H. Leckie, *Authority in Religion*, pp. 56, 57, 119, 120, 130, 135, 139, 142, 143, 222–224. (T. & T. Clark, of Edinburgh.)

APPENDICES

JOHN HENRY NEWMAN

B. MODERNITY *VERSUS* MODERNISM

APPENDIX A[1]

JOHN HENRY NEWMAN [2]

I

" Uneasy lies the head that wears a crown."
Trite is the maxim ; but life makes truisms
original by turning them from abstract to concrete. Of no concrete instance could these
words be truer than that of the great Oratorian
and Cardinal, who has found in the son of his
disciple and adversary so skilful a biographer.
The crown of gifts and of influence was Newman's in a shining splendour, not often granted
to the *littérateur*. Gifted with an intellect subtle
and logical, with force and culture, with a soul
sensitive " to the best that is known and thought
in the world," with a sympathetic insight into
human nature, and a clinging tenderness, and
withal an inward fire alike of faith and passion
which flamed out, at times in wrath and at others
in appealing eloquence, he is a king of controversialists no less than among sermon-writers. He
had a command over the English language un-

[1] Reprinted from the *English Church Review* for March and
April 1912.
[2] *The Life of John Henry Cardinal Newman*, by Wilfrid Ward,
(Longmans, Green & Co. 2 vols.)

equalled in our literature, and could be pathetic, ironical, or enthusiastic at will, or drop into a breezy directness and a very definite humour, while at other times he seems to touch the very depth of the human spirit, or to rise with an awed solemnity that is almost supernatural. But this is not all. Of all the men of the Victorian age, none was more universal or had a wider influence, or was more fruitful of ideas and principles which still endure. It may be doubted whether any contemporary has made more difference than John Henry Newman. At the lowest estimate, he changed the whole face of things in the English Church, and left marks on her that are indelible. But this was the least of his achievements, and others had more part in it. His act in 1845—that great going out—had, for its issue, a change in the attitude of the English people towards the Roman Communion. He widened the range of possibilities for all educated men, and largely altered the sympathies of the uneducated. It is not in the least that the English nation shows any sign of submitting to the see of Peter, or that many people do not still hate Rome, and perhaps more fear her. But he brought it all into the open, just as it has been pertinently remarked that he helped to make modern Oxford by giving her a hold on the public interest which she has never since lost. If men hate and fear Rome, they do so no longer as an open enemy, but as a present risk, an awful but unwelcome possibility. Rightly or wrongly, Newman's act, with its resulting series of apologies, has changed the way in which everyone interested regards the possibilities of religious change. He has made possible, at least in imagination, an alternative which was not possible before he lived and wrote, and could not have been made possible by all the other " converts " apart from him. Further than this, he has altered the whole tone of the country in regard to Popery. Englishmen may remain sound Protestants, or Pagans, or Positivists, or Agnostics ; but none of them regard " the grim wolf with privy paw " in quite the same light as their fathers did. They cannot do so. Bluster as they may, they can no longer picture a Papist as " a sort of creature," as Walter Bagehot once wittily put it.

Other causes doubtless contributed to this end. One of them is the growth of intellectual anarchy, and the habit of playing with any and every form of religious allegiance, which, so far from being due to Newman, was his *bête noir*. Nor did he effect his results in isolation. Nobody does. A man is great because he is the leading spirit of a general movement. Even in his more arduous later work, it need not be questioned that other men, some of them Newman's antagonists, Wiseman, Manning, W. G. Ward, and even Faber, bore their part, a part by no means small, in working the change. But to allow all this is only to allow what is true of any leader of opinion. What can be said is that while it

would have made little difference to the total
result if any of the others had done nothing, it
would have made the whole difference if Newman had not been what he was. If neither
Ward nor Manning had ever lived, the change
would have differed but slightly; if Newman
had never lived, it would (humanly speaking)
have never taken place at all. To him, more
than to any other cause, or group of causes, is
due that change in the general atmosphere which
is still proceeding. Newman found and fixed the
interest of the " great " public, even when they
least agreed with him; and he attained an eminence shared by none among his Tractarian or
Roman colleagues. This fact was shown in the
remarkable outburst that ensued on his death :
an outburst so general that it stimulated the
malign activities of one learned antagonist, who
waited till he was safe from reply before beginning
his polemic. Evidences both intellectual and
practical abound on all hands, which show that
his influence is still proceeding in a way which
can hardly be said to be the case with Pusey or
Keble or even Church, and is certainly not the
case with Ward or Manning.[1] Over the determined hostility of the latter to his cherished
plan of allowing Roman Catholic youth an
education at Oxford and Cambridge, Newman
triumphed, though not in his lifetime. He

[1] Certain recent developments seem to show that the conceptions of " Ideal" Ward are once more having great influence
with a certain section of Churchmen.

seems to have felt that his principles, like all far-reaching and revolutionary ideas, could have their fruition only in the future. On one point he said in a letter to Manning, " I write this as a protest and an appeal to posterity." This notion explains the somewhat meticulous care in which, feeling wasted and useless, a broken man, he spent much of his time, during the sadder years before the final recognition, in docketing and arranging his papers ; that men might have due means of justifying not only his devotion and his orthodoxy, but also his acumen and statesmanship. This justification is now complete, or nearly so, in the volumes before us. Mr. Ward has done his work with admirable skill, and with a devotion to the great Oratorian, which yet never fails in respect to his own father, Newman's only worthy antagonist ; while he is scrupulously loyal to the former Cardinal Archbishop of Westminster. Possibly the general reader may think that too much space is occupied with the details of long-buried controversies, and that more might have been made of the inward and devotional aspects ; but this complaint would hardly be fair. So much has already been made public on these matters ; so bitter are still some of the antagonisms, that it was but right that a reasonably complete account of them should be given to the world ; and less than we have would have been to have given the game into the hands of the enemy.

This being so, and the issue of those debates

being for the nonce what it was, it is not surprising that a certain grave melancholy seems
to pervade these volumes. All the Tractarians
indeed were touched with an almost Puritan
gloom, and had little of that boisterous gaiety
which is the note of some of their successors ;
and to the last Newman, it is said, remained in
ἦθος a Tractarian. But it is not this of which
the reader will think. It is the prevailing note
of melancholy, the sadness which comes of contemplating great powers very largely wasted.
Of this waste the subject was fully conscious ;
and the relatively small output of work from
1860 onwards is its clear proof ; for the *Apologia* was a *livre de circonstance* written at
lightning speed, and the *Grammar of Assent*
could have been followed up by many other
volumes had Newman felt sure of sympathy,
or even of reasonable fairness, on the part of
authority. As he says in one place :

" I come more to see than I did what an
irritabile genus Catholic philosophers are : they
think they do the free Church of God service by
subjecting it to an etiquette as grievous as that
which led to the King of Spain being burned to
cinders." And in another, " Now I think that
the iron has entered my soul." It is not indeed
for us to throw stones, for in that incomparable
sermon on the Parting of Friends, no passage
was more poignant than the sentences in which
he set out his grief at the consecrated stupidity
which reigned in official precincts of the English

Church, and led to the refusal and the repression of the noblest activities of her servants :

" O my mother, whence is this unto thee, that thou hast good things poured upon thee and canst not keep them, and bearest children, yet darest not own them ? Why hast thou not the skill to use their services, nor the heart to rejoice in their love ? How is it that whatever is generous in purpose, and tender or deep in devotion, thy flower and thy promise, falls from thy bosom and finds no home within thine arms ? Who hath put this note upon thee, to have ' a miscarrying womb and dry breasts,' to be strange to thine own flesh, and thine eye cruel towards thy little ones ? Thine own offspring, the fruit of thy womb, who love thee and would toil for thee, thou dost gaze upon with fear, as though a portent, or thou dost loathe as an offence ;—at best thou dost but endure, as if they had no claim but on thy patience, self-possession, and vigilance, to be rid of them as easily as thou mayest. Thou makest them ' stand all the day idle,' as the very condition of thy bearing with them ; or thou biddest them be gone, where they will be more welcome ; or thou sellest them for nought to the stranger that passes by. And what wilt thou do in the end thereof ? . . ."[1]

Newman's troubles in the Church of Rome were in one sense surface troubles. He at no time had that doubt about her claims or exist-

[1] *Sermons bearing on Subjects of the Day*, pp. 407, 408 (ed. 1885)

ence which united with official neglect to drive
him from the English Church. Yet these words
might not unfitly describe his sense of the
attitude of the official and conservative elements,
Propaganda and its meaner servants in England,
towards nearly every project that he took up,
and all the ideas which he deemed most fruitful
—except, of course, in the final years. Some
indeed have dared to claim that, so far from
neglect, Newman met with a recognition almost
without parallel, and that the alleged ill-treatment was the mere figment of a morbidly
sensitive self-love.

To refute such a claim it is enough to recall
the facts. From the very first period of his
visit to Rome, before he had even founded the
" Oratory," Newman was misunderstood and
thwarted. Ordered against his will to preach,
he offended authority by taking too high a tone,
and was thought for once to have been not
liberal enough. He complains already of " too
much of an iron form at Rome " ; and the
great argument of the *Development of Christian
Doctrine* was regarded with suspicion.

Permitted to establish the Oratory, and afterwards the school, at Edgbaston, he was thwarted
in every other undertaking, and deliberately set
tasks which were impossible. Even the school
seems to have been merely tolerated ; and the
Fathers were at one time afraid that the authorities would order it to be stopped.   Glad enough
of his conversion, those authorities were not so

ignorant of England or of Newman as not to hope much in the way of brilliant society successes; but of the real work of educating the minds of his co-religionists, and of creating a Catholic atmosphere in the world of thought, they were jealously suspicious. They understood but little of his aims and insight; of what they did understand they disapproved. The evidence of this is scattered all over these volumes, and is partly to be found in other works. The scheme of a Roman Catholic University in Dublin (as it was projected by Cardinal Cullen) was hopeless from the first. Newman was entrapped into it, and there never seems to have been any attempt to treat him fairly or even with decent courtesy. The Cardinal managed to frustrate the positive promise of a bishopric *in partibus*, which should give him a *status*, and communicated it to him in ways deliberately insulting. But, indeed, the ideas of the two men were irreconcilable from the outset; and no courtesy could have led to any but a temporary appearance of harmony. Newman wanted a real university; the Bishops, a mere clerical seminary, with the professors, as he put it, " simply scrubs." " On both sides the Channel, the deep difficulty is the jealousy and fear which is entertained in high quarters of the laity. . . . Nothing great or living can be done except where men are self-governed and independent; this is quite consistent with a full maintenance of ecclesiastical supremacy. St. Francis Xavier wrote to Father Ignatius on his knees;

but who will say that St. Francis was not a real
centre of action ? " [1]

In these sentences he lays down the true principle of authority. But it never was, and never
will be, understood at Rome, whose doctrine of
authority is that of sovereignty, held by the
jurists of the Roman Empire.

Not only, however, did failure foredoom the
Irish expedition to extinction, except that in the
Idea of a University and the less-known *University Sketches* we have some compensation,
" the perfect presentment of a theory " in Pater's
view. Far worse was the treatment of Newman
in England. Cardinal Wiseman's culpable negli-
gence led to the disaster of the Achilli trial.
The verdict, however, like other misfortunes,
proved a blessing in disguise ; for, being in the
teeth of all the evidence, after a scandalous
summing up by the Judge (Campbell) it led to a
revulsion of feeling, and that beginning of shame
for the " no Popery " prejudice, which Newman
afterwards turned to so good account. For
there can hardly be much doubt that this incident, seemingly so adverse, prepared the way
for the very different treatment accorded to
Newman by the public in the controversy with
a more distinguished adversary. " This Kingsley business," as Manning scornfully termed it,
is so well known that nothing need be said of
it here, except to express the hope that we may
ere long be given a complete edition of the

[1] Vol. i. p. 367.

"*Apologia*," *including the preparatory pamphlets.*
They are admirable reading, and it is a nuis-
ance not to be able to obtain them except at a
fancy price. They are also good evidence of the
depth of unfairness, if not of positively disingenu-
ous writing to which an able man like Kingsley
could descend; in the confident belief that " any
stick was good enough to beat a Papist with."
Mr. Ward has earned our thanks by reprinting
from the Appendix Newman's answer to the
absurd allegation of Kingsley, that because he
had declared Christian living to be a certain
note of monastic life, he therefore denied it was
to be found anywhere else. Dr. Abbott, in one
of his attacks on Newman's memory, went so
far as to justify Kingsley on the ground that
when I ask, " Where shall I find the book if
not on the book-shelf ? " I certainly mean it is
not on the table. The cases are obviously not
parallel. The one case is purely singular, the
other universal. If a particular article is in one
place, it is not in another. Not so with a
moral or spiritual quality. If I ask, " Where
shall courage be found if not in the British
army ? " does anyone suppose that I mean it is
not found in the German army or the navy or
the public schools ? The point is important,
for it illustrates the blind prejudice which mis-
leads even able men when the Protestant bee is
in their bonnet.[1]

[1] Another even worse instance occurred in the same discussion. In reference to Newman's view, that we must believe

One other fact comes out in Mr. Ward's account of the *Apologia*. It was literally a book written with blood and tears. Its poignancy is due not so much to literary genius as to the terrific tension both of body and mind with which it was produced. He wrote for sixteen, even twenty-two, hours at a stretch, his hand so tired at times that he could not write without pain. Here is a pathetic letter to Hope-Scott :

"MY DEAR HOPE-SCOTT,—What good angel has led you to write to me ? It is a great charity.

"I never have been in such stress of brain and such pain of heart,—and I have both trials together. Say some good prayers for me. I have been writing without interruption of Sundays since Easter Monday—five weeks— and I have at least three weeks more of the same work to come. I have been constantly in tears, and constantly crying out with dis- tress. I am sure I never could say what I am saying in cold blood, or if I waited a month ; and then the third great trial and anxiety, lest I should not say well what it is so important to say. Longman said I must go on without break if it was to succeed,—but, as I have said, I *could not* have done it if I had delayed.

on merely probable evidence, his assailant declared that prob- ability means provableness, and that no educated man nowa- days believes that religion is demonstrable. It is difficult to find words in which to describe such quibbling. It is more than twenty years since the writer read this debate, and at that time he was an agnostic; yet his memory of the impression then made of unfairness is still vivid.

"I am writing this during dinner-time,—I feel your kindness exceedingly." [1]

No wonder the book is what it is, if that was the state of its author. The letter is worth quoting, for it is an illustration of that style called " transporting " by Mr. Gladstone—for once in his life a good critic. It is the amazing intimacy and depth, the head of a man with the heart of a rather little child, that makes Newman's style appealing beyond other writers : all this, added to that strange touch of the other world which hangs like a cloud over all his utterances.

But although the *Apologia* won back for Newman a public popularity at a time when his name was almost forgotten and his books had ceased to sell, it did not appease the narrow and contemptible official *camarilla*, who were envious of his greatness. Manning disliked " the fuss Oakeley makes about it," and was much disturbed by the laymen's letter of respect. It was this address which drew from the egregious Talbot that masterpiece of epistolary composition which illuminates, as by a flashlight, the mind of the mere official in the Church and in many other institutions : " Dr. Newman is the most dangerous man in England. . . . What is the province of the laity ? To hunt, to shoot, to entertain." [2] Perhaps in no single phrase has the utter collapse to which Christianity comes in the

---

[1] See Ward's *Life*, vol. ii. p. 25.   [2] *Ibid.*, vol. ii. p. 147.

worldly-minded been more perfectly exposed.
The whole of the Christian revelation has come
to mean that the members of the Church, except
a small official class, may " entertain." Imagine St. Paul or St. John preaching to that
worthy end ! It is even better, in its way, than
the epigram Disraeli put into the mouth of one
of his men about town : " What on earth could
he want to go to Jerusalem for ? I am told
there's no kind of sport there." It is one of
the tragedies of human life that men of Newman's calibre should not infrequently be at the
mercy of persons like this Court-flatterer.[1] Nor
need we suppose that their activity is confined
to the Roman Communion.

At the same time, Newman was no " plaster
saint," nor was he easy with people. Even in
Pusey's *Life* there are hints of a suspicious
irritability. Those who held a brief against
him have at least this upon their side ; Newman
was hypersensitive, was ready to imagine slights,
deeply resented all unfairness, had an over-
accurate memory for injuries, and a pen not
dipped in oil. To the same Monsignor Talbot,
who wrote and asked him quite politely to
preach a course of sermons in his church at
Rome, Newman sent this curt answer :

" DEAR MONSIGNOR TALBOT,—I have received
your letter, inviting me to preach next Lent in

[1] More of Monsignor Talbot's letters are to be found in
Purcell's *Life of Manning*, vol. ii. He went mad (unfortunately)
later.

your church at Rome to ' an audience of Protestants more educated than could ever be the
case in England.'

"However, Birmingham people have souls;
and I have neither taste nor talent for the sort
of work which you cut out for me. And I beg to
decline your offer.—I am, yours truly,

"J. H. N."[1]

No one could deny to Newman the power of
expressing what he felt or that he could see,
through the thin veil of courtesy, the enemy and
the backbiter; but it can hardly be said that
a reply so *farouche* was necessary, or even
Christian. The truth is that those who yielded
to his own wishes and his mother's fears, and
saved him from the knocking about of a public
school, probably did him a deeper injury than
any among his numerous adversaries. Newman's sensitive temperament might not have
allowed him a happy life at school; but he
would have had a far happier manhood and old
age if he had roughed it as a boy. A spirit so
delicate and subtle, with fibres so minutely
attuned to catch impressions, could, in any case,
only do its work through suffering; it is the
prize of genius, the crown of thorns of the born
artist. This could under no conditions have
been avoided; but his sheltered youth made
his after-troubles all the more poignant, and
rendered him needlessly *difficile*.

[1] Ward's *Life of Newman*, vol. ii. p. 539.

It is the merit of this biographer that, while
quite clearly he is full of sympathy and admiration for his subject, he does not in any way
attempt to minimise this trait in Newman, or
to make him out as perfect. He gives full
weight to the less pleasing characteristics. At
the same time, despite his well-meant efforts,
Mr. Ward has not succeeded in removing the
impression created by other sources about
Manning's attitude towards his quondam leader.
True, there was a clear difference of policy ;
and Manning doubtless believed it right to
withstand some of Newman's projects. But,
though Mr. Ward has strained some doubtful
points and set the best face possible upon
some others, an English Churchman has no call
to admire the Cardinal Archbishop except in
the Latin sense of the term. In my judgment,
based mainly on the documents in the second
volume of Purcell's *Life of Manning*, the
Cardinal was moved very largely by personal
motives. Mr. Purcell may not have been a
very fair critic, but no one, so far, has accused
him of forging the documents in those volumes ;
and the evidence of the letters, and still more
the diary and self-criticism at the end,[1] are
almost overwhelming proof that Manning was
not altogether unconscious of Newman's intellectual superiority, and was jealous of it. Nor
again does Mr. Ward really succeed in removing
the impression that Manning tried, by an in-

[1] See *op. cit.*, vol. ii. chap. xiv., especially pp. 346–351.

genious trick which was very nearly successful, to prevent Newman from obtaining the Cardinal's hat. Mr. Ward admits that Manning disregarded Ullathorne's direct statement that Newman's letter meant only that he wanted a Papal dispensation from residence at Rome. With this fact and others printed elsewhere it is not easy to understand how anyone can say that Mr. Ward's book puts an end to this notion.

Nor, again, does it appear other than probable that part of Manning's opposition to Newman's darling project of a house or college at Oxford was due to the desire to keep him in obscurity, in the sense that Newman at Oxford would far overshadow any other Roman in England, even were he Archbishop. I do not say that this can be proved ; but it falls in with the notion which Manning gives us of his own character, with Newman's notion of it, and with the common opinion, for which there is plenty of evidence.

The one man whose opposition to Newman was always disinterested was W. G. Ward. This appears never to have been questioned. No characteristic of these volumes is more praiseworthy than the combination of skill and fairness with which the author treats of the long duel between his father and his hero. A duel there certainly was. On Ward's side it was conducted with a good temper, in direct proportion to the violence of his language. He never lost his reverence and even love of his

old master ; and he spoke of himself as intellectually homeless without his support. Newman
was never able to treat this conflict so coolly. To
the last his tenderest affections gathered round
" the city of the dreaming spires " ; and he felt
acutely the evil which Ward had worked by his
controversial virulence, besides the bar to his
own work set up by this antagonism.

That Newman's position was, in the nature
of the case, a difficult one is most clearly shown
in other matters. The long-drawn agony of the
Rambler and the *Home and Foreign Review* has
had its story told elsewhere by Dr. Gasquet.[1]
For all that, Mr. Ward has been well-advised
in devoting several chapters to this topic. It
has been the writer's fortune to go through a
mass of unpublished correspondence on this
matter for a different purpose ; and I can 'he
more heartily testify, not only to the wisdom
of Mr. Ward's selection, but also to the fairness
of spirit in the whole narrative. What emerges
clearly out of this long and complicated network
of negotiations and ventures is this :—Newman
tried to be fair to both sides ; he succeeded,
and, in consequence, received the customary
reward. He was loyal to the English Bishops,
who did not understand the situation with which
Acton and Simpson were dealing. On the other
hand, he was not unsympathetic with the highly
conscientious school of young writers who were
set on bringing their co-religionists in England

---

[1] See Gasquet, *Lord Acton and his Circle :* Introduction.

up to the level of cultivated Europe. Both parties complained of Newman. With neither was he in full agreement; neither trusted him, though both tried to make use of him for their own ends, and wanted the help of his great name. Both of them thought Newman had left them in the lurch. Neither was right. In his loyalty to the Bishops, and to that principle of authority in which he vitally believed, Newman did his best to temper and control an enthusiasm which was sometimes almost indecent, often ill-advised, and rarely self-restrained in its expressions about the history and hierarchy of the Church. In his loyalty to truth and to the modern spirit, he did his best to secure these young men a "run for their money," and he succeeded. He took credit to himself, quite justly, that it was he who, by taking over the *Rambler*, however reluctantly, served the hierarchy; for only so was it got out of the editorial hands of Richard Simpson. And Simpson was the *enfant terrible* of the party; as Newman put it in a letter to Acton:

" I must, though it will pain you, speak out. I *despair* of Simpson being other than he is. He will always be clever, amusing, brilliant, and *suggestive*. He will always be flicking his whip at Bishops, cutting them in tender places, throwing stones at Sacred Congregations, and, as he rides along the high road, discharging pea-shooters at Cardinals who happen by bad luck to look out of the window. I fear I must say

I despair of any periodical in which he has a part. I grieve to say it, but I have not said it till the whole world says it. I have, I assure you, defended him to others, and it is not many weeks, I may almost say days, since I was accused of 'solidarity with the *Rambler*.' But what is the good of going on hoping against hope to the loss of union among ourselves, and the injuring of great interests ? For me, I am bound to state my convictions when I have them ; and I have them now.

" You will act with true sincerity of intention and with full deliberation, whatever conclusion you come to about the *Rambler ;* but I don't think Protestants ought to say that an independent organ of opinion is silenced, but one that loved to assail, and to go out of his way to assail, what was authoritative and venerable." [1]

On the other hand, by his short-lived connection with the *Rambler*, and by the fact that in some sort the *ægis* of his sympathy was thrown over the Liberals, he enabled them to keep the review going (in one form or other) until 1864, when Acton stopped the *Home and Foreign Review* in order to forestall an official condemnation. It is evident from the correspondence that each party tried to use Newman entirely as its own instrument, and to use the whole of him ; while he insisted on being himself, and would not surrender at discretion to either.

[1] Ward's *Life*, vol. i. p. 529.

It was during this episode that he contributed to the *Rambler* the famous article on " Consulting the Laity in Matters of Faith." This was deported to Rome by some officious prelate, and did Newman untold harm in the eyes of the clique represented by Talbot. Yet this article—which, unfortunately, is not reprinted— is to a modern reader the wisest and most profound defence possible of the principle of religious authority, and at least gives suggestions as to its true nature, which is not always understood even by English clergymen. For Newman never made the cardinal error of confusing the Church with the clergy. He discerned the true basis of religious authority in the whole community, its root in the natural sociality of man. He argued for authority on the only grounds on which it can in truth defend itself ; and his article should be compared with the admirable chapter in Mr. Arthur Balfour's *Foundations of Belief*.[1] What was (and we suppose is) hidden from the official *camarilla* was the fact that it is only through this liberalising apologetic that the Church can hope to make any stand against the " sea and the waves roaring, and men's hearts failing them for fear " of modern infidelity. What, on the other hand, was hidden from the rasher liberals like Simpson and Acton was the essential justice of the claim to authority, and the need of tact and measure in expressing new truth. Thus for Newman it was a case of

[1] *Op. cit.*, chap. ii. part iii.

getting all the kicks and none of the halfpence. This is still his case. There are people still to be found who maintain Carlyle's "rabbit" theory of his intellect, merely because he resisted the prevailing rationalism. Others again see in him the dangerous originator of ideas, exhibited in their naked futility by extreme Modernists. But Newman was neither of these things ; his was the most subtle, acute, and sympathetic mind which devoted itself to the problem of religion as a whole in the nineteenth century. Impressed at once with the duty and the difficulty of defending the Christian life as the most reasonable view, he saw the need of understanding its adversaries, and of using the appropriate new weapons. Archery is no longer of service, now that gunpowder has become general. What he did was to introduce gunpowder into apologetics—and thus to originate a vast movement in the direction of definite faith—and to provide new weapons more appropriate than the outworn scholastic long-bow. But of this more in a later article.

Newman, however, was, above all things, himself : not a philosopher, nor a saint, nor a controversialist, nor a preacher, nor a poet, in the sense that implies a type. He was, emphatically, John Henry Newman, the most winning, and withal imperious, of men ; and the personal touch is never absent from his writings, all of which may be treated as the *glossa ordinaria* to which the *Apologia* forms the text. He said of himself that he had not the gift of rule. This is true; but he had, in a very high degree, that other gift of all real leaders, the power of attaching men to himself—and that, though he seems to have been hampered by an almost painful shyness. Perhaps this is why he wrote so well. The reticent man can express himself more readily on paper when he is not face to face with his interlocutor. Thus it is true, as Mr. Ward said earlier in an admirable study, that the key to his work is found in the words, " *Cor ad cor loquitur*." One instance may be given. It is the more noteworthy that the persons in it are both members of the Oratory. Father Philip Gordon had been meeting Newman daily for some weeks, and could not comprehend why he never spoke to him. Thinking he must have offended, he was astonished one morning by Newman putting into his hand the following letter :

" MY DEAREST BROTHER,—It is strange to write to you and write about nothing ; but such is my fate just now and for some time, that, since I have nothing to say to you, I must either be silent or unseasonable.

" Many is the time I have stood over the fire at breakfast and looked at you at Recreation, hunting for something to talk about. The song says that ' love cannot live on flowers ' : not so, yet it requires material, if not for sustenance, at least for display—and I have fancied

too that younger and lighter minds perhaps
could not, if they would, care much for one who
has had so much to wear him down.

"All blessings come on you, my dear Brother
—in proportion to my waning." [1]

Clearly a nature so reticent as this with his
intimates would not find it easy to explain itself
to suspicious outsiders. The touching chapter
on "Life at the Oratory" shows him at his
best, and will be full of interest to English
readers. The most illuminating incident in the
whole book is, however, the account of Newman's final relations with Mark Pattison. Years
ago, I remember noticing how in the *Memoirs* [2]
(when are we going to have the second part ?)
the grim Rector of Lincoln, while he speaks
with a sort of cold rage of the whole Tractarian
Movement (of which for a short time he was an
adherent), makes one exception. He never
mentions Newman without a tone of respect,
and almost of reverence. How deep that feeling
was is shown by this most remarkable incident.
When Pattison was on his death-bed, Newman
wrote to him, and ultimately paid him a visit.
His first letter received the following reply :

"When your letter, my dear master, was
brought to my bedside this morning and I saw
your well-known handwriting, my eyes filled so

[1] Ward's *Life*, vol. i. p. 204.
[2] *Memoirs*, by Mark Pattison (Macmillan & Co., 1885).

with tears that I could not at first see to read what you had said.

" When I found in what affectionate terms you addressed me, I felt guilty, for I thought, would he do so, if he knew how far I have travelled on the path which leads quite away from those ideas which I once—about 1845–1846—shared with him ?

" Or is your toleration so large that, though you knew me to be in grievous error, you could still embrace me as a son ?

" If I have not dared to approach you in any way of recent years, it has been only from the fear that you might be regarding me as coming to you under false colours.

" The veneration and affection which I felt for you at the time you left us are in no way diminished ; and however remote my intellectual standpoint may now be from that which I may presume to be your own, I can still truly say that I have learnt more from you than from anyone else with whom I have ever been in contact.

" Let me subscribe myself for the last time
" Your affectionate son and pupil,
" MARK PATTISON." [1]

This is the only revelation in the book. It adds more to our knowledge of Pattison than of Newman. Excellent and well-arranged as is this biography, and however admirable the selection of letters, it does not materially alter

[1] *Ibid*, vol. ii. pp. 481, 482.

our conception of its subject; nor was this to be expected. The *Apologia*, the letters published in Manning's *Life*, and the two volumes of correspondence edited by Anne Mozley, his works, and the accounts of Church, Froude, Shairp, Arnold, and others, had brought Newman so near to us, that we could not suppose that even the official biography could do more than deepen the impression and fill in the details. I doubt even if this book will change men's judgments of Newman. His lovers (and they are many and devoted) will find in them fresh sources of admiration, new grounds for judgment of his adversaries. His enemies (and they are far from dead or quiet) will proclaim more loudly than ever that he was an impossible person, difficult and hypersensitive; that he has been honoured for the wrong reasons; that the respect of Englishmen of all creeds and classes is a measure of his disloyalty to the Papacy; that his apologetic is dangerous and revolutionary. That it is revolutionary, I do not deny; as to its being dangerous (except in the sense that all courage is dangerous), I would, so far from allowing, assert, on the contrary, that it is the sole method likely to be of service in the struggle before us.

Perhaps the most useful impression left upon the general reader will be an insight into Roman official ways. The book will show, if the Encyclical *Pascendi* and its accompaniments have not shown it already, how strangely they de-

ceive themselves who think that, exchanging
" the Anglican paddock " for the Roman *cam-
pagna*, they exchange slavery for freedom.
Whatever may be the defects and difficulties of
our English Church, " its freezing coldness " in
parts, its smug officialism, the complacent
atmosphere redolent of the cathedral precincts
and the clergyman's wife :—all these things,
which stank in Newman's nostrils, may still, in
some sense, be with us. We may still have
much to learn from Rome in regard to the place
of the poor in the Christian Church, and the
recovery of many things which have nearly
vanished under the arid tyranny of the *Aufklärung*. For all that, this book demonstrates,
what the recent condemnation of Mons. Duchesne
has set in clearer light, that the actual working
of the Vatican machinery is controlled by a
narrow and jealous *camarilla*, as incapable of
generosity as it is ignorant of true religion.
Unworthy to black the boots of a man like
Newman, they did their best to shut his mouth.
The tragedy of Newman's life—and it was a
tragedy—is the tragedy of the saint and the
genius, thwarted by the spirit of worldly
officialism and unsympathetic autocracy. But
it is a deeper tragedy even than that. It is the
tragedy that is the well-nigh inevitable destiny
of any man, fundamentally conservative in his
religion, yet open to all the intellectual and
literary currents of his time. Such a man is
always supposed by unbelievers to be more

conservative than he is, and to mean by his words what he does not mean. He is scorned as a mere traditionalist, obscurantist, and so forth. On the other hand, mere orthodoxy condemns his dangerous liberalism and discerns risk in his knowledge of modern scepticism, and wants to be told in three words why we cannot be content with the arguments that did duty in 1680. That is the real tragedy of Newman. However vehemently we may blame Roman stupidity, or Manning's jealousy, or the Jack-in-office insolence of Talbot, it remains most true that such a temper as Newman's, and such an attitude towards " things new and old," are at once the only wise method, and are yet inevitably fruitful of difficulty and misunderstanding in any branch of the Church and in any period of history,—certainly not least in our own branch and in the present century.

II

The Apologist

Mr. Ward's merits as a biographer have been deservedly extolled. All that need be said of this book in this regard is said, if we describe it as worthy of the *Life of Cardinal Wiseman*, and the two volumes on *W. G. Ward,* and the *Ten Personal Studies*. Although, however, the personal side of biography is its most salient feature, and the cause of its popularity with the general reader, it is not all. In the case of a man so intimate in his expression and even so personal in his thought as Newman was, this side is obviously central ; yet it is not on this side that the distinctive quality of these volumes lies. Other biographers might have equalled Mr. Ward in descriptive portraiture ; for his writing, though subtle and penetrating, is never compelling. It interests the reader rather than grips him. Another might have imitated that self-restraint which prevented him from making a *succès de scandale*. This would not have been a very easy task, in view of the acute differences which Newman always encountered, and his own intense feeling. Probably only those who know the inner history of the time can rightly appraise that mingled loyalty and skill which has made these volumes illuminating, while preventing them from being outrageous. But these are gifts which, though rare, are not precisely striking ; and another might have done as well—or, possibly, even better—on the devotional side.

But what Mr. Wilfrid Ward has given us, and what nobody else could have given us with the same security, is the portrait of Newman as an Apologist. There, we are convinced, was his outstanding gift ; this it is which marks him off from Keble and Pusey, and even from Church. Into this went all his insight, all his elasticity and the penetrating subtlety of a nature at once deeply religious and profoundly sceptical —in the technical, not the popular sense. This

Q

is what ranks Newman beside Pascal in the modern world. This it is which Mr. Ward has so vividly presented to us. No other person could have had the same qualifications. He has done good work of his own on these lines ; no one knows better than the founder of the Synthetic Society the need of adequate intellectual equipment, if the Church is to hold her own amid the welter of moral and religious anarchy in which we live. Versed in the conversation of the modern world, intimately acquainted with every eddy and current of philosophical and historical criticism, Mr. Ward feels the danger now, as Newman felt it long ago. One of the most interesting, perhaps quite the most important, passage in the two volumes is the account of his visits to the Cardinal, and the discussion of this very problem. A paragraph must be quoted which shows how free Newman was from the dangerous error of basing one's arguments on the practical earthly value of the Christian Faith. This is true to a certain point, but it always breaks down in the long run ; and, when men find that it affords no guarantee towards making the best of this world, they are apt to drop the Faith.

" ' I could talk to you for half an hour,' he said, ' on the common sense of worldliness and the folly of other-worldliness. This life is secure and before us. The Christian ideal of life is disproportionate to our nature as we see it. It is based on unreal enthusiasm. Let us make sure

of what is before us. Let us perfect our nature
in all its aspects and not give the abnormal
and unnatural preponderance to the ethical aims
which Christianity demands. We speak of our
nature as testifying to Christianity. But is this
true ? Is it not only a mood which so testifies ?
Does not the calm, sober study of mankind and
of human nature *as a whole* lead us to wish for
a *mens sana in corpore sano,* a nature healthy
and well developed in its artistic, its intellectual,
its scientific, its social capacities, as well as in
its moral ? Is not the ideal Christian life a
very risky venture, based perhaps on a conclusion due to prejudice and fanaticism ? This
is at least too possible a *hypothesis* to make
it wise to venture all in the supposition that
Christianity is true and give up the certain
pleasures of this life for what is at best so
uncertain.' " [1]

He then goes on to develop the perfectly
sound argument that miracles are precisely the
same instance of the power and freedom of a
spirit or spirits outside this world as are the
actions of man ; while the point put to him by
Mr. Ward about the " naturalist " contention,
that man's action occurs only within nature, and
that the case is therefore not parallel, only
makes it clearer than ever that the objection to
miracle is precisely of the same nature as that
to human freedom. Determinism is fatal to
both ; and, either to determinism or else to

[1] Vol. ii. chap. xxxiv. p. 492.

denial of a world of active spirits beyond this, the impugner of the miraculous on *a priori* grounds is always brought at last. This is what Newman appears to have seen, and to have argued with his wonted skill.

Another point, very favourite with the Cardinal, appears in the course of this conversation : viz. the danger of proving too much.

" ' I would be very particular,' he said, ' in pressing on the attention of the young men, the *nature* of the proof they are to expect on religious subjects. They must not expect too much. Butler somewhere compares the imperfection of the religious argument to the imperfection of a ruined castle. In many cases the shape of the castle is quite as clearly determined by the ruin which remains as it would be were the castle whole. And so with the proofs of natural and revealed religion. There is enough capable of expression to indicate the *shape* and *character* of the proof, though it is in detail very imperfect.' " [1]

But not only is Mr. Ward fitted by his personal tastes and intellectual affinities to appreciate the true character of Newman's work ; as the son of W. G. Ward, he knows, by deeper means than those of reading, the state of the cultivated world at the time when Newman began his self-imposed task. He could see what Newman in his earlier days was " up against," in a more vivid light than that vouchsafed to

[1] Vol. ii. p. 495.

most men of a later generation.   Moreover,
though Ward and Newman were deeply divided
on ecclesiastical politics and the method of
presenting the solution, they were agreed on
fundamentals ; for Ward, no less than Newman,
understood the danger, and was largely at one
with him as to the means of meeting it philo-
sophically.   Ward, for instance, reviewed with
applause the *Grammar of Assent;* while, on the
other hand, Newman, as he used to say, was
in agreement with him at bottom.   He was, as
his critics have pointed out, in spite of his
alleged " minimising " tendencies, and his un-
doubted " inopportunism " in 1870, always an
Ultramontane.   So, we should suppose, is Mr.
Wilfrid Ward.   Indeed, if any single man could
be said to be the intellectual heir of Newman, it
must be generally admitted that Mr. Ward has
a good claim to that title.

It is in the emphasis so justly laid on this side
of Newman's work, so near his heart, and in the
full account of its development and detail that
the main merit of this book lies.   The task
which Newman had set himself he defined in the
" *biglietto* speech " which he made after receiv-
ing the cardinal's hat :

" ' To one great mischief I have from the first
opposed myself.   For thirty, forty, fifty years
I have resisted to the best of my powers the
spirit of Liberalism in religion.   Never did Holy
Church need champions against it more sorely
than now, when, alas ! it is an error overspread-

ing, as a snare, the whole earth ; and on this great occasion, when it is natural for one who is in my place to look out upon the world, and upon Holy Church as in it, and upon her future, it will not, I hope, be considered out of place, if I renew the protest against it which I have made so often.

" ' Liberalism in religion is the doctrine that there is no positive truth in religion, but that one creed is as good as another, and this is the teaching which is gaining substance and force daily. It is inconsistent with any recognition of any religion, as *true*. It teaches that all are to be tolerated, for all are matters of opinion. Revealed religion is not a truth, but a sentiment and a taste ; not an objective fact, not miraculous ; and it is the right of each individual to make it say just what strikes his fancy. Devotion is not necessarily founded on faith. Men may go to Protestant Churches and to Catholic, may get good from both and belong to neither. They may fraternise together in spiritual thoughts and feelings, without having any views at all of doctrines in common, or seeing the need of them. Since, then, religion is so personal a peculiarity, and so private a possession, we must of necessity ignore it in the intercourse of man with man. If a man puts on a new religion every morning, what is that to you ? It is as impertinent to think about a man's religion as about his sources of income, or his management of his family. Religion is in no sense the bond of society.

" ' Hitherto the civil power has been Christian. Even in countries separated from the Church, as in my own, the *dictum* was in force, when I was young, that " Christianity was the law of the land." Now, everywhere that goodly framework of society, which is the creation of Christianity, is throwing off Christianity. The *dictum* to which I have referred, with a hundred others which followed upon it, is gone, or is going everywhere ; and, by the end of the century, unless the Almighty interferes, it will be *forgotten*.' " [1]

In a letter written in 1874, Newman writes :

" I think our Lord's words are being fulfilled, ' When the Son of Man cometh, shall He find faith upon earth ? ' The plague of unbelief is in every religious community : in the Unitarian, in the Kirk, in the Episcopalian, in the Church of England, as well as in the Catholic Church. What you want is faith, just as so many persons in other communions want faith." [2]

It is this perception of faith as the real need which, on the one hand, defined Newman's attitude towards Rationalism, and, on the other, led him to his peculiar method in apologetic : a method conservative in essence, and revolutionary in form. That is " the mystery of Newman," as M. Bremond called it. What makes him so difficult a puzzle, and gives him so compelling a charm ? How could a mind, in some respects so modern, so sensitively attuned to every breath and current of opinion, and

[1] Vol. ii. chap. xxxiii. pp. 460, 461.
[2] Vol. ii., Appendices, p. 566.

open to all, or most, of the avenues of modern
knowledge, be content to take up a position
which seemed the negative of everything
modern ? He is rightly regarded as the source
of Modernism, in the sense that he discarded
the scholastic method of proof, and as the
originator of a doctrine of development without which it is not really possible to justify the
Church. What he actually did was to bring
religion under the category of life, instead of
treating it as an aggregate of propositions to
which assent is demanded on grounds intellectually coercive. But Newman, as the passage
quoted shows, was in no sense a Modernist, if by
that be meant one who is content with only
the present value of a system and confuses its
truth with its worth, or one who treats as of
slight importance the historical character of the
New Testament narratives.

Another point is to be noted. Although Newman developed, he did not alter. In 1845 we
find him writing, " For years I have an increasing intellectual conviction that there is no
medium between Pantheism and the Church of
Rome " :[1] a statement which events have served
to render still clearer, if we substitute for
" Rome " the word " Catholic." Indeed, it is
abundantly evident from this book that,
although in theory Newman may have been
Papalist, he never shared the notion of government which is inherent in the Papal Curia ; nor

[1] Vol. i. p. 81.

was it that element that really attracted him. It
was the Catholic religion, the great human-divine
thing, the collective conscience of humanity,
the central fact in spiritual experience, with its
majesty of immemorial tradition and the pathos
of a million tears, the great community of the
saints, and the martyrs, and the mystics, and
the sinners, with its roots in the past and its
strong social bonds : that was the really compelling charm to a man of Newman's temperament. Little wonder that, things being as they
were, he could find this only in the Roman
obedience ; but for us, on whom a brighter day
has dawned, things need not be so. Newman's
general view, then, alike of the need and the
way to meet it, remained unchanged. His
views in the *University Sermons*, and still
more clearly in his first visit to Rome, are
very near those of the *Grammar of Assent*,
and the conversations with Mr. Ward. It has
been maintained that to the last Newman
retained the $\mathring{\eta}\theta\mathrm{os}$ of the early Tractarians.
Whether or no this view be well grounded, there
can be little doubt that, on the most fundamental
problems and the nature of their solution, he
altered hardly at all from what he held in
1843. What he saw in his earlier days he
still saw later. But he saw it with increasing
clearness of detail ; and before he died it was
also seen by most people interested in the intellectual aspects of Faith. That is the point.
To us it may seem only natural that a man

placed as Newman was should write as he did
in 1845; it is hard for one of this generation to
see how much insight was needed to say what he
did then. Assailed by clamorous infidelity, and
equally clamorous fancy religions, living subsequent to the great vogue of naturalism, we are
little likely to deny the fact of the " Armaged-
don," which is the present condition of the
Church in the world. It is plain as the sun at
noontide. It is insinuated in our novels, argued
in our reviews, personified in our drama, chat-
tered at our dinners, propagandist in our
universities. The present writer was ordained
deacon in 1894; at that time he was wont to
say that, unless he had information to the
contrary, he never expected an educated layman whom he met casually to be a Christian in
belief. Such a view was the natural result of
the conditions of the *fin de siècle*. But Newman
began his work in the Oxford of William IV.
Even now there are many circles in which this
view of the crisis would be deemed outrageous.
If you take the atmosphere of a provincial
cathedral close, or of most rural deaneries in
country districts, it may be doubted whether
its tone of complacent optimism would think
that there was anything worthy of serious
thought in modern infidelity. Unbelief in such
a view is a sort of freak, a fad—like wearing
sandals—so far as practical work goes, a phenomenon so rare as to be negligible. Even among
those who ought to know better, problems of

Church policy and even of faith are often treated as though it were all a sort of squabble in the family, and there were no Goths thundering at the gates. If this be still the case to-day, we may judge how hard it must have been to see the facts in 1832. One claim of Newman on our gratitude is that he saw the danger much sooner than other people, and was ready to meet it. Of course, it had been seen on the Continent. Chateaubriand, De Maistre, to say nothing of Lamennais, were fully aware of the state of things. The French Revolution had secured that. It was, indeed, one of the services of Newman that he brought England into closer touch with the movement that was sweeping over Western Europe. As Dr. Barry has so brilliantly shown us in his little book on Newman,[1] the Oxford Movement was but the English aspect (and not all of that) of that romanticism which displaced the *Aufklärung* in the imagination of Europe, and paved the way for, and indeed created, modern Ultramontanism. This movement had important consequences in many fields not religious. Its vogue was due to many causes. There was the weariness induced by the arid and superficial rationalism of the eighteenth century; the revival of the historic sense, " the passion of the past "; the growth of nationalism with its sense of a hyper-individual and hyper-logical unity in the life of great peoples; the feeling that beauty and its

[1] *Newman*, by Dr. W. Barry, in *Literary Lives* Series, edited by Sir W. R. Nicoll (1904).

expression meant far more than mere immediate
utility in the life of the world. In religion a
world which devoured Victor Hugo, and had
been nurtured on Scott and La Motte Fouqué,
and lived after Shelley and Keats and even
Byron, could not fail to demand something
warmer and fuller of colour than the cold
moralities of Liberalism, and of something more
full of social and sacramental symbolism than
mere Evangelicalism. At the same time, it
was the Evangelical Movement, with its keen
sense of the supernatural and its intensely personal reality in religion, that prepared the way
for it. In form the Tractarian Movement was a
reaction against Simeonism ; in reality it was
its fulfilment. Each of them was a protest in
behalf of a vital religion against the mere respec-
tabilism of preachers like Blair. Each was full
of the other-worldly reference as against the
mainly civic and social notions of the Arnoldians.
Not, indeed, that this latter element was want-
ing to either. The Evangelical Movement,
however recluse and Puritan its notion of social
life, generated in its earlier days a very real
social enthusiasm. It was William Wilberforce
who abolished the slave trade ; as it was Lord
Shaftesbury who fought and won the battle of
the child in the factories against tremendous
odds, including the interested opposition of
plutocratic friends of the people, and the inhuman theories of doctrinaire economists, at that
time justly named " the dismal science."

I need not go into the services rendered by the Oxford Movement to social reform. They are not the least salient of its results. Then, as always, it has been the mystic, the man with his eyes on the other world, whose hands are most forward to do good in this. If anyone needs proof of this, let him compare recent addresses of the Bishop of Oxford with the utterances of certain dignitaries confessedly " liberal " on all subjects connected with the poor. It is not the sacerdotal or mystical temper which complains of the effort to secure a decent wage and housing for his fellow-countrymen as looting. Mere intellectualism in religion, so far from producing characters like Mrs. Humphry Ward's " Richard Meynell," an essentially melodramatic figure,[1] has always had a certain Sadducean aristocratic tinge, alike in the *abbé philosophe* of the eighteenth century, and in the drawing-room divine of later days.

Newman himself is an admirable instance of the growth of Evangelicalism into the richer life of Catholic Christianity, and of the profound connection between the two. At the present moment we witness such phenomena as the Student Movement, with delegates from Cuddesdon and Kelham and Mirfield mingling with other Christians, of the World Missionary Conference, with its S.P.G. representatives, and the increasing number of Conventions of church-people of all

[1] See *The Case of Richard Meynell*, by Mrs. Humphry Ward (1911).

parties. It would seem idle to deny that the
two parties are being drawn together, however
reluctantly. If, as we hold, Evangelicals have
much to learn from the greater fulness of the
Catholic life and its insistence on the social and
sacramental aspects of religious experience, we
need not deny that many who glory in the name
of Catholic have little less to learn from the
real faith in the Cross and personal devotion to
our Lord of the true Evangelical. Perhaps there
is no more soul-destroying superstition than the
dilettante Catholicism to which religion is no
more than ritual ; and, even short of this, there
is an arid scholasticism too often masquerading
as faith, or adopting a line purely legalist and
conservative. What the two parties are at
bottom opposed to is that negative individualist
spirit, " the all-dissolving, all-corroding scepticism of the intellect," as Newman calls it,
which would eviscerate Christianity of all its
distinctive charm. If it be true that there are
two, and two only, mutually exclusive views of
life, the Pantheistic and the Christian, it is not
surprising that all who hold to the latter should
be forced by the immanent logic of this principle and the presence of the attack into something like unity ; while, on the other hand, the
man who is a " liberal "—and nothing more—in
his view of history, of miracles, and of grace, is
being forced more and more down an inclined
plane into some form of Pantheistic idealism.

It was Newman's distinction to have per-

ceived this crisis in its earliest stages. Casting
about as to methods of defence, he soon learnt
that he could not cope with the evil by mere
subjective pietism, or even by Evangelical orthodoxy. He felt the need of some great collective
union to withstand a spirit so universal and so
alluring. Further, he recognised the need of
restating those elements in the Established
Church which had been left untouched by the
Evangelical Movement. In view of the fight
before us, a faith that is mere acquiescence
and a practice that is no more than conventional
are of no avail. They crumble (and since then
they have crumbled) the moment a serious
enemy assails them. Then, as now, it was true
that the fire of faith and the flame of sacrifice
alone can preserve religion, ever more encom-
passed by the armies of the alien. This is what
drove Newman to Catholicism. His further
move into the Papal Church was largely due to
the same cause. His sensitive and impatient
temper could not away with the complacent
banalité of the official Church of England, her
" freezing coldness," as he called it. Fortunately, that is largely changed now ; and, in so
far as it is not, Rome will go on winning converts from among us.

When Newman had gone to Rome, his task—
that of furnishing the educated mind of Europe
with a philosophy of belief—was still unfulfilled.
This apologetic, while it should in no way ignore
or minimise the assured results of history and

of science, should keep in the main to the old spirit, " changing that she might remain the same." His aim all along was conservative ; his method was revolutionary. His view throughout is so well known that a very brief account of it will suffice. The University Sermons, the *Development of Christian Doctrine*, the final section of the *Apologia*, and the *Grammar of Assent* are the works in which his thought works itself out most systematically ; although, in the case of a writer so personal and intimate, there is hardly anything he wrote but bears the traces of it.

First of all, the method of demonstrative logical proof is definitely abandoned. In this he followed Butler, and, of course, Kant ; though he seems not to have read the philosopher of Königsberg till quite late in life. Newman was content to argue that, since all action is founded on probable reasoning, and what man needs in religion is moral certainty, *i.e.* a certitude that would justify action, a cumulative argument is the most appropriate and is sufficient. Certitude in spiritual things is moral certainty, and not mechanical inference. Further, he saw that in order to justify the developed scheme of Catholic theology, something more than logical argument is needed. This he found in the fact of life. His development of doctrine is an essay in creative evolution. It seeks to show that, since life is ceaseless movement and energy, we must apply dynamics rather than statics to our criticism of the Church. All that the inquirer needs is to satisfy himself that the Church, as she now appears, is the actual development of the Christian society of early days : that it is but the oak of which the meeting in the upper room was the acorn. I think that it is not always clear whether Newman intended by his development a truly " creative evolution," or merely the explication necessary to the original idea. Tyrrell charged against him the narrower view. But although, writing when he did, he may well have confused the two, his whole temper made in favour of that view of the life of the Church as essentially creative, with which M. Bergson has made us all familiar in regard to the universe as a whole. In spite of its defects and the looseness of the tests he applies, Newman's *Development of Christian Doctrine,* together with Möhler's *Symbolik,* remains a most valuable asset of Catholic apologetic.

But Newman went further than this. In the *Grammar of Assent* he analysed the act of belief, and went on to show, that far more than mere formal logic is involved in every real assent. The doctrine of the illative sense may or may not be well-expressed ; but it does express the truth that all living belief is a reaction of the whole personality upon the material presented, and that it cannot be interpreted by the external methods of rationalism. Moreover, it is obvious that, if the logical faculty be inadequate, the collective voice of the community

R

will find its place. On no purely intellectualist system is it possible to justify religious authority, except in the sense that a mathematician might use it of the conclusions of an expert who had gone further. But religious authority is a deeper thing than this ; it is not a formula which enumerates conclusions logically demonstrable. It is the life of the whole spirit-bearing body, which its members share like an atmosphere or a language,—occasionally, though rarely, coming to articulate statements or creeds.

This notion of authority is perhaps more clearly expressed in the *Rambler* essay on " Consulting the Laity." It attaches itself to nearly all the more modern appeals to authority. An excellent justification of it is given in the chapter on " Authority and Reason " in Mr. Arthur Balfour's *Foundations of Belief.*[1]

This brings me to another noteworthy point. Newman had the future on his side. He seems to have felt that his work would fructify after he had gone. We may regret the incompleteness of his writing, and lament the local and personal forces that hindered him from working out his ideas ; but we can hardly deny that what Newman did has paved the way for all the more recent developments of the philosophy of religion. All that is of lasting value in the pragmatist criticism of truth can be found in Newman, although he was never a pragmatist

[1] See above, p. 233. A recent work which is of much value in this regard is *Authority in Religion*, by the Rev. J. H. Leckie.

in the strict sense. He knew that truth was apprehended by the whole man, not merely by the reasoning faculty ; but he would never have said that truth was nothing more or less than value, or that you could go on believing, say, in God, although you had no notion that there was anything objective to answer to the belief. In the same way, his doctrine of development points yet on to that conception of evolution with which M. Bergson has " taken the town." Newman's surrender of the attempt to base religious belief on proof intellectually coercive has been the commonplace of nearly everything the writer has ever heard or read on the subject ; *e.g.* such a very different work as Westcott's book, *The Gospel of Life.* Newman, indeed, did not originate this view ; but he made it far more widely prevalent than before, and he analysed the grounds for it. But when all is said, it is his introduction of the category of life and his conception of the religious society as an organism that will probably remain his most enduring contributions. This it is, more than anything else, which entitles him to be called original, and has brought him an influence out of all proportion to those who read his books. He is not the mere obscurantist upholder of tradition because it is tradition that he is sometimes deemed to have been :—a reproach which, not unjustly, clings to some of his party. His ideas have so deeply permeated the thought and feeling of the age that his books are less

read than they ought to be. His principles
have become so general that the author is sometimes forgotten. Another instance is Tract 90.
The outcry which it provoked was terrific;
but it may be doubted whether any thinking
man in the Church—Sacerdotalist, Liberal, or
Evangelical—can justify his subscription, except on the principles of that pamphlet. The
ethics of conformity is a confessedly difficult
problem; but certainly some of the party
loudest in condemnation of Newman's ingenuity could have been able to justify their
own adhesion to the Church only by a liberal
expansion of the same principles.

What the services of Newman have been to
the cause of religion it is perhaps too early to
determine; certainly I shall not seek to do so.
This much, however, may be said. He pointed
the way which all must follow who have the
same cause at heart. He discerned the true
state of the case at a time when it was hidden
from the vision of most, and not easily seen
in orthodox churchly Oxford. He saw that
rationalism could have but one end, even
though, in individuals, it might be devoted to
the service of orthodoxy. He saw that individualist religion would soon become merely
a subjective sentiment, as has since proved the
case with the development of undenominationalism; that a strong, collective authority was
needed, instinct with the Holy Spirit imparted at
Pentecost. He felt that Christianity, as being

a life, not a theory, was a distinct thing, and must be judged as a whole, not by the meticulous criticism of details. He discerned that the real problem concerns the total nature of that religious fact which stretches from the priest at the Eucharist (for we must begin there) back through the Church to the New Testament experience. The problem is whether or no this fact is supernatural, *i.e.* whether it be the uprush of the spirit of man towards the secret of reality, or whether it be the down-coming of God to man. He felt that, once that total supernatural character be accepted, all the rest will fall into its place. Thus he quite rightly defended the so-called ecclesiastical miracles, as against Protestant orthodoxy, which, while it does not deny miracle, yet makes it more difficult of credit by confining it to a very thin space of years; while his sense of the Catholic Church as the central thing in the spiritual life of the race enabled him, in the *Essay on Milman's View of Christianity*, to prepare the way for the modern recognition of many non-Christian elements in the Catholic cult.

Finally, and this is of the utmost importance, Newman wrote in order to be read. Deserting the academic for the popular style, he was able to do far greater work than the mere *savant* who writes only for other scholars, and abhors style as a diabolic temptation. Newman's *Grammar of Assent* can be read with interest by any man who cares for good writing and ingenious argument. It was so read by the writer of this article at a time when he had no thought of taking Holy Orders and no interest beyond the literary. It is to be wished that Newman's example could be taken to heart by some of those who are writing on the same topic at this moment. Now more than ever is it needful to have books—the work of learned men, as in the case of Newman,—which shall get free from all dullness and use every possible means of persuasion, wit, sarcasm, eloquence, colour, good writing. Why should it be supposed that a pompous condescending style is likely to convert people, or that the devil will be scared by books written like the works of the late Mr. Justice Chitty ? Charm of style is a quality by which even unbelief loses all its grossness. Dullness has not yet been raised to the rank of a theological virtue, though it seems too often to be the chief virtue of theologians. These remarks may seem impertinent, for the writer has never been more acutely conscious that his work is below the level of its subject. But writing is a difficult art ; as Mr. Tulliver said to his wife, " talking's puzzling work." Nobody can do more than try his best. Too much of the writing on theological topics reads as if the authors were trying to do their worst.

APPENDIX B

MODERNISM *VERSUS* MODERNITY

THE preceding lectures were delivered in the spring of 1913. They were in print some time before the appearance of the *Open Letter* of the Bishop of Oxford. Since then, the topics dealt with in the last lecture have received a great deal more illustration. It seems well to say a little more about them. Two points in particular seem to need further elucidation;—(*a*) the ethics of conformity, and (*b*) the integral character of miracle in the Christian outlook.

I. THE ETHICS OF CONFORMITY

No one can consider this topic as easy, or as admitting of rough and ready standards. None of the numerous pamphlets that have appeared seems to make it incumbent to change what I have written in the text. In *The Miracle of Christianity*, the Lady Margaret Professor at Cambridge puts in an eloquent plea for an interpretation of the Creeds which shall be religious rather than legal or historical. This claim need not be taken to deny the wisdom of that warning since issued by the Bishops of the Province of Canterbury ; nor do I understand that Dr. Bethune-Baker denies its wisdom. On the other hand, those who disagree with the opinions of the " liberal " clergy ought at least to make efforts to understand that revolution in the whole mental standpoint which makes this position seem natural to those who hold it. For it is a revolution ; and it involves more than some of the critics of " liberalism " appear to realise. Not merely is it the case that all of us nowadays interpret symbolically certain phrases in the Creeds which our ancestors interpreted literally. All that may be covered by the distinction made by Dr. Gore between faith in matters dealing directly with the other world and faith in facts which, if they took place at all, took place in this world. That is not the difficulty. The difficulty is deeper in import. It is this. Many other statements occur in the formularies which relate to events professedly historical. Yet most of us, even those farthest removed from any standpoint rightly termed Modernist, can use the words relating to these (alleged) events only with mental reservation. What may be the ultimate judgment of history about the Deluge or the Passage of the Red Sea or the Sinaitic revelation, I suppose no one can say. Probably no certain knowledge will ever be reached. But this much is certain. We do not consider it as essential to sincerity that a priest, when using the Baptismal Office, should take the story of Noah in a literal sense ; or that, when celebrating the Eucharist, he should hold as historical fact the traditional account of the giving of the law. In such matters latitude is claimed and allowed by all—except indeed by the few survivors who still hold to verbal inspiration, or at any rate to the historical accuracy of the early Biblical narratives. But once this principle is allowed, it alters the whole way in which men look at the obligation of formularies. All that the liberals are doing is to claim to press this to its extreme conclusion.

What is claimed by the liberals (who are erroneously termed " modernists ") is to apply to some of the historical statements in the Creed the same principles of interpretation we all of us apply elsewhere. We may not think that they are right ; but can we say that their claim involves insincerity, so long as they tell us what they mean ? The great name of Henry Sidgwick has been invoked on this side ; but this name has no terrors. Henry Sidgwick is a very interesting example of the Cambridge mind in the heyday of Victorianism ; and he wrote the epilogue to the work of Bentham and the Mills. Yet his was a mind of very distinct limitations, and extraordinarily meticulous. That he should have been anxious to tie the clergy down to a literal belief in any item of the Creeds is in accordance with the individualistic and rather academic tone of his thought ; but it is no more decisive of the question than was the view of Huxley that Christians were bound, on pain of insincerity, to believe that the world was made in six days.

Each of us may feel that if he were to come to hold such views, he would not be able to go on acting as a priest; but we may hold that in many other matters. So far as I understand them, if I were to come to the position of certain *soi-disant* "Roman" Catholics in the Church of England, the only course open to me would be that of making my submission to the See of Rome; but these men do not think this. I do not call them insincere, however little I feel that I understand them. To take another instance; many a High Churchman may feel that the doctrine of "the real absence" proclaimed by certain extreme Low Churchmen would not for him be compatible with the office of a priest in the Church of God. They, however, do not feel this; and few of us, I suppose, would charge them with dishonesty. Why, then, are we to talk of insincerity (however much we may dislike it) if a man claims to minister in the Church while rejecting the ordinary sense of certain statements in the Creeds? Some, indeed, may go a great deal further than the position taken up by Dr. Sanday and Dr. Bethune-Baker; others may employ their intellectual gifts in disguising their negative opinions, hinting at their true beliefs rather than stating them. Of such we need say nothing. But what the liberals by their accredited spokesmen appear to be claiming is this, that they believe what the Creeds taken *as a whole* mean, and that you cannot take them except as a whole. They are organically related to the whole life of the Church ; they state, or try to state, its spirit ; and the act of their recital must be judged in relation to the whole organic life of the Church and the individual member. Most of them would probably accept *ex animo* that summary of the Apostles' Creed which is given in the Church Catechism :

" First, I learn to believe in God the Father, who hath made me and all the world.

" Secondly, in God the Son, who hath redeemed me and all mankind.

" Thirdly, in God the Holy Ghost, who sanctifieth me and all the elect people of God."

It seems, then, that we may dislike the views of the " liberal " clergy ; that we may hold that they will naturally lead on to a very much more negative position ; that we may do all we can to withstand them, or to prevent such persons being ordained or promoted. One thing we had better not do ; and that is, raise the point of honour, or say that anybody who says the Creed in this way is promoting insincerity.

Here we are met with the reply, " You are ignoring the significance of Credal Affirmation. The Creeds stand on a different footing from the rest of the formularies. They express the mind of the Christian Society, and are intended to express it." I agree. They do. The Liturgy is an act informed by the Christian spirit, not a statement of Catholic belief. The Creed is.

Further, it is said, "A man's assent to the Creeds is not merely social; it implies the individual's own adhesion." It does. I cannot think tenable that position taken up some years ago by Dr. Sanday with regard to the Athanasian formula: "It is not I, but the Church, that says the Creed." Surely it is both. Or rather it is Dr. Sanday as a willing member of the Church; and he is not justified in using the Creed, unless he is able to say this much : " I believe the Church to be the society for promoting God's will. I accept as a part of its discipline the obligation to recite these words, as an alternative to the greater evil of refusing to minister in that society." Even this, however, seems to be too little. A priest ought to be able to feel of the doctrinal clauses this much at least. They are an expression of the mystery of our Lord's Personality. This expression may be inadequate, but it is truer to assert it than to deny it ; for it guards against theories which, if logically developed, would destroy faith in that supernatural fact, "the great mystery of godliness." Even of the warning clauses I think that a man should feel that they assert the possibility of the salvation of the intellect, and that therefore, however crude their form, they are a safeguard against (a) that rationalism which refuses to see any use for faith in so far as the operations of the intellect are concerned, and thus subjects men to its tyranny as to a machine; and against (*b*) the more prevalent heresy that denies the intimate relation between belief and life. To deny the Athanasian Creed at this moment would inevitably be held to mean that (i) we no longer hold to the mystery of our Lord's Person; (ii) that the intellect can work purely by itself and can neither be helped nor hindered by the Spirit; and (iii) that creed and character have nothing to do with each other. However that may be, I do not deny that the Creeds stand in a different position from the other formularies, or that adhesion to them involves an individual, no less than a social, loyalty.

All, however, that that comes to is this. A man must satisfy his conscience that in using the Creeds he is meaning what they mean; not necessarily what each item means, but what the Creeds mean as a whole, and as expressing the corporate mind of the Church as interpreted and illumined by all its life and its liturgy, of which they are a part. When, however, a man comes to a different view from mine as to what that meaning is, I cannot see how I am to judge of his sincerity. So many factors combine; and the emphasis, the values of each part, vary for every individual so greatly that each person must make his own harmony out of all.

For the truth is that we have changed. The atmosphere in which we debate these matters is not what it was. As I should put it, our conception of credal affirmation is more Catholic, less individualist than it used to be. Our sense of the greatness and wonder of that life which inspires the Christian community has made it less possible to treat its formularies in a purely analytic spirit—adding up its articles of faith like items in a banker's ledger. Is there not borne in upon each of us, whether conservative or liberal, the sense that loyalty to a great religious society with a complex organisation and a long past is not the formal acceptance of so many propositions, and that it depends upon what sense we put upon the whole, what value we give to each of the parts ? Loyalty to the idea of the Church, to its living Lord, to its earthly membership, to its multitudinous life, to the many-coloured richness of its sanctity, to the romance of its origin, to the treasures of its present inheritance, but above all loyalty to the splendour of its future glory ;—that is the root of the matter. When a man feels that he has that, who are we that we should lightly charge him with dishonour, merely because he applies in one place methods of exegesis which each one of us applies elsewhere ?

Finally, it must be said that this *apologia* for those from whom the writer differs depends upon one condition. That condition is as follows. The priest who wishes to act on the principles here laid down can do so, only if he is loyal in a high degree to the corporate and social life of the Church—as were the Roman Modernists. Persons who belittle the institutional side of religion hardly seem entitled to put forward this plea of benefit of clergy.

II. THE CRITICAL MIND

All this, however, makes it more needful to set forth those limitations of the " liberal " mind which rob its pronouncements of persuasion for many men not unreflecting.

In the first place, it should be noted that the burden of proof falls upon those among Christians who advocate this " reduction." As believers in the Incarnation and the Blessed Trinity, the most eminent of the controversialists have come forward; and they are appealing to those like-minded. Those who are asked to surrender, as " over-beliefs," things hitherto regarded as integral to the faith, while told to remain Nicene Catholics still, are bound to examine the grounds of this challenge. Unless there should be, not merely a doubt but something almost overwhelming, those who are not mandarins will be wise if they stand to the old ground that the two elements in the Creed are inseparable in practice, whatever they may be in theory. Have the utterances of modern liberal critics that quality which gives them an indefeasible claim to our adhesion, or can we discern, in their general outlook, elements which arouse a certain distrust ?

PRESUPPOSITIONS

Dr. Sanday makes it apparent that the difficulties in the way of accepting the traditional accounts lie in the region of presuppositions. The objections are *a priori ;* they are not in the evidence itself, any more than they have always been.

No occurrence recorded in the New Testament is attested by weightier evidence than the feeding of the five thousand. That, we are now told, must be explained as a Eucharistic myth, on the ground that it involves something *contra naturam.* Does it ? How do we know that ? As Professor Gwatkin says, " Can anything be said to be *contra naturam,* except a contradiction in terms ? " To assume that any alleged event is *contra naturam* is to assume that we know all about Nature and that we can treat it as a closed system. The whole contention of Theism rests on the denial of this.

Moreover, the moment we begin talking of Nature, it is very important that we should bear in mind that Nature is a human name given to certain aggregates of facts ; also that it is used in many different senses. Half the difficulties raised on the topic of miracles arise out of a confusion between two or more of these senses ; such a confusion appears to be made in the contrast drawn by Dr. Sanday between events " *supra* " and events " *contra* " *naturam*. This has been remarked by the Dean of Christ Church.[1]

Nature may be used to denote the nature of things. No miracle can be contrary to this. The value of miracles to those who credit them arises from their revealing the nature of things by a flash, and from their preventing any superstition that it is merely a mechanism.

Nature is often used, as by Huxley and St. Augustine, in the sense of all that happens. Here, again, miracles, if they take place, are natural ; nothing *contra naturam* is even conceivable. It is in the literal—not the journalistic —sense unthinkable. Sometimes, again, Nature is used to mean the whole phenomenal world. This also would include miracles, if there be such ; for *ex hypothesi* miracles are occurrences in the visible universe. Changes, however catastrophic in the inward life, need not, except in figure, be termed miraculous.

Sometimes Nature is used to denote that part of existence which can be rigidly expressed in mechanical formulæ. In this sense, a miracle is supernatural ; but so also is any human act which involves freedom. So also, in all probability, are many biological processes, and important steps in the history of life ; that is, if the scientific man of to-day is to be trusted.

[1] See Strong, *The Miraculous in Gospels and Creeds*, pp. 20–22.

S

More and more does it appear to be the view of science that the Spencerian notion of evolution is not borne out by the facts ; that the laws of matter and motion are not of themselves suffi-cient to account for chemical—and still less for biological—facts.[1] M. Bergson is the greatest, but by no means the only, influence which has substituted a doctrine of evolution which is creative, for one which is merely mechanical. This doctrine shatters all the old objections to miracles, as indeed is mournfully admitted by some of the " liberals." In this view freedom is seen, not at one or two points but at many. The problem indeed is the old one between freedom and mechanical necessity. Even John Stuart Mill in his *Essays on Religion* adduced the analogy between acts of human and acts of divine freedom. Now that more is known of the course of physical development, those outside scientific circles will feel less disposed than ever to surrender at discretion to a mechanical con-ception of evolution. *We are not going to do it.* Yet, of all this movement many of the liberals seem ignorant ; and others, less creditably, seem suspicious. In another regard, that of varia-tion and discontinuity, the words of Mr. W. Bateson in his presidential addresses to the British Association give furiously to think.

[1] *Cf.* Prof. J. A. Thomson's two articles, " Is there One Science of Nature ?" in the *Hibbert Journal* (Oct. 1911 and Jan. 1912); and Dr. J. S. Haldane, *Mechanism, Life and Personality* (Murray, 1913).

The following passage from a popular work by one of our most distinguished men of science is evidence of the distance we have travelled since the days of Huxley and Spencer; it is taken from the *Introduction to Science* of Prof. J. A. Thomson :

" Consider, for a moment, a famous passage " from Huxley : 'If the fundamental proposition ' of evolution is true, namely, that the entire ' world, animate and inanimate, is the result of ' the mutual interaction, according to definite ' laws, of forces possessed by the molecules which ' made up the primitive nebulosity of the uni- ' verse ; then it is no less certain that the present ' actual world reposed potentially in the cosmic ' vapour, and that an intelligence, if great enough, ' could from his knowledge of the properties of ' the molecules of that vapour have predicted the ' state of the fauna in Great Britain in 1888 with ' as much certitude as we say what will happen ' to the vapour of our breath on a cold day in ' winter.'

" This very strong and confident statement " appears to us to illustrate the need for philo- " sophical criticism.   As Bergson points out, it " denies that time really counts ; it also denies " that organisms are more than mechanisms. " It denies the creative individuality of the " organism, which trades with time in an unpre- " dictable way all its own.   It may be right in " these denials, but the points are arguable. " Moreover, the general idea of evolution does

" not warrant us in supposing that intelligent
" behaviour, for instance, ' reposed potentially
" in the cosmic vapour ' and could be predicted
" from a ' knowledge of the properties of the
" molecules of that vapour ' ; for molecules and
" the like are abstractions of physical science
" which, for the purposes of that science, may be
" treated as if they represented the whole of the
" reality.   The ' primitive nebulosity of the uni-
" verse ' was a reality which, for the purposes of
" physical science, would be analysable into a
" whirling sea of molecules, but that certainly
" cannot have been the whole truth about it if in
" it there reposed potentially the present actual
" world.   To take an analogy from development,
" there is no reason to believe that we should
" have exhausted the reality of a human ovum
" if we knew all about the properties of its proteid
" molecules, nor that we could predict from
" that knowledge whether the ovum would
" develop into a genius or a fool." [1]

This notion that the nature miracles are
contra naturam in any sense that makes them
incredible seems to rest partly upon a wrong conception of our knowledge of nature, and partly
upon a misleading use of two other terms that
have been imported into these discussions,
viz. " law " and " order."

Law is a term that has been borrowed from
jurisprudence by natural science, in order to
express the generality of certain sequences in

[1] In the *Home University Library* Series, No. 32, pp. 142–144.

Nature as observed by man. Unfortunately, this term "law" has been—and still is—understood as though it meant a necessity imperatively imposed by an Omnipotent Fate. So far from this being the case, natural law means only that as we have observed them things do happen in these sequences. These laws are not, like the laws of mathematics, necessary deductions from certain given notions. When science speaks of observed uniformities, it cannot say more than this :—that if certain forces go on operating, certain other results will follow, provided no new cause is acting. Even this may be too much, as M. Henri Poincaré pointed out.[1] "Grâce à "la généralisation, chaque fait observé nous en "fait prévoir un grand nombre ; seulement nous "ne devons pas oublier que le premier seul est "certain, que tous les autres ne sont que prob- "ables. *Si solidement assise que puisse nous* "*paraître une prévision, nous ne sommes jamais* "*sûrs absolument que l'expérience ne la démentira* "*pas, si nous entreprenons de la vérifier.* Mais la "probabilité est souvent assez grande pour que "pratiquement nous puissions nous en contenter. "Mieux vaut prévoir sans certitude que de ne "pas prevoir du tout."[2]

In all the matters under discussion the contention is that new forces were operating. The uniformity of nature would be violated by

[1] Even here, however, M. Poincaré has shown how much of choice is involved in current notions of space. See his two books, *La Science et l'hypothèse* and *La Valeur de la Science.*

[2] *La Science et l'hypothèse*, p. 171.

such facts as Our Lord's Birth and Resurrection, only on these conditions; either that these were mere freak events without any adequate cause, or that they had produced no corresponding results. Precisely the contrary is the case. That is why the existence of the Christian Church must ever play a large part in the argument.

Nor again is it easy to understand on what ground the alleged miracles are said to be " one little submerged rock in the beautiful sea of order." Miracles are not, and are not by the wildest fanatic supposed to be, contrary to the order of the universe. If they were, they would have no meaning. The order of the universe as a whole is the only real order; the mechanical order, except on a materialistic theory, is but a formula for a part of it. Miracles reveal the personal, as distinct from the mechanical, nature of the universal order. On that ground it is not even wise to say that miracles might not be predicted.[1] Since they are in accordance with the " determinate counsel and foreknowledge of God," persons with spiritual insight may be able to foresee them— although such gifts will be found in circles other than the studies of academic critics. So

---

[1] See *La Science et l'hypothèse* and *La Valeur de la Science*, e.g. such passages as this in the latter (p. 95): " Tout ce que nous "pouvons dire c'est que l'expérience nous a appris qu'il est "commode d'attribuer à l'espace trois dimensions." In this connection, special reference may be made to the two chapters on *La Notion d'Espace* and *L'Espace et ses Trois Dimensions*.

far from miracles being contrary to order, they are in the highest sense expressive of order ; for they are admittedly irreconcilable with a mechanical conception of the universe. Ultimately a mechanical universe would not be an orderly one ; for order is a spiritual quality.[1]

All *a priori* difficulties about miracles have vanished before a creative conception of evolution. Yet the writer is free to confess that much needless trouble has been caused by the Protestant attempt to deny their occurrence at all times save in one short period. On all hands evidence is accumulating which will persuade all but the prejudiced of the truth of the Catholic conception of miracle, as a peculiar power of being or beings, either here or beyond, in living union with God— which, so far from exhibiting itself at one time only, has been exercised in all ages of the Church, and probably also of human life. Ever since the seventeenth century, naturalism has held so strong a sway in Western Europe, that it has been more and more difficult to win attention for such alleged facts ; where mentioned, they were treated as vulgar superstitions. Modern tendencies have reacted against this tyranny. Telepathy (which cannot be explained on a naturalistic basis[2]), faith-healing, levitation, and many other facts are now before us. True,

[1] *Cf.* on this point Mr. T. J. Hardy, *The Religious Instinct ;* the chapter on " Miracle " is perhaps the best in this most stimulating and illuminating work.

[2] *Cf.* on this point a valuable article by Mr. Gerald Balfour in the *Hibbert Journal* for April 1913.

men still differ as to the amount of credence
which they afford them. This much, however,
may be said. Most of us would approach the
stories that gather round the figure of a Father
John of Cronstadt in a spirit very different
from what would have been deemed possible to an
educated person fifty, or even twenty, years ago.
So far, indeed, as concerns much that is now
stirring, it is not unlikely that the Christian
Church will suffer attack on the ground that
it makes too little rather than too much of the
miraculous. Westernism is not Christianity ; and
the East, which we have so long despised, has
already begun to take her revenge.

How can knowledge of the laws of nature
forbid us to believe this or that, if these laws are
no more than a description of what ordinarily
takes place ? For some time, scientific men
have been dinning into our ears that these
laws give only general *formulæ*, descriptive
of the physical world ; that they tell us the
" how " of things, and have nothing whatever
to say concerning the " why." It is only if we
know the " why," as well as the " how," that
we can say whether such an occurrence as
the miraculous birth of our Lord is ruled out ;
certainly we do not as yet know any grounds
for dealing with it in this way.[1]

[1] The following passage from M. Poincaré seems to show
that part of the difficulty arises from the continued rule of the
notion of the natural order, as it was conceived by the ancients :
" Comment l'ordre de l'univers était-il compris par les anciens ;
" par exemple, par Pythagore, Platon ou Aristote ? C'était ou

Many grounds indeed there are for asserting its likelihood, under the conditions. The
individual, the unique, the surprising variation,
the new beginning, non-repeatability of events;
—these are the things which more and more we
hear of. Now the point of the Catholic contention is that the birth of Jesus Christ was the
most wonderful of all new beginnings. What is
there difficult in supposing that its wonder
should have touched the physical, no less than
the spiritual, sphere ? Is not the contrary view
more difficult ? Does it not lead us to a view
of physical nature as something apart from
God, instead of seeing in its laws the expression
of His will, which is living? It is to cut the
world in twain to assert that so mighty a change
as the Incarnation must involve no physical
disturbance. Such a view treats the moral and
spiritual as being alone the sphere of Divine
activity and leaves the physical separate.
Assuredly there is some ground for connecting
this view with that " false spiritualism " which
is a denial of the principle of Incarnation.

" But," it will be said, " that is precisely
" what you orthodox are doing : you are assert-

"un type immuable fixé une fois pour toutes, ou un idéal dont le
"monde cherchait à se rapprocher. C'est encore ainsi que pen-
"sait Képler lui-même. . . . C'est Newton qui nous a montré
"qu'une loi n'est qu'une relation nécessaire entre l'état present
"du monde et son état immédiatement postérieur. Toutes les
"autres lois, découvertes depuis, ne sont pas autre chose, ce
"sont, en somme, des équations différentielles." (*La Valeur de
la Science*, pp. 162, 163.)

"ing a harsh dualism, and denying the blessed "truth of the Divine Immanence." Far from it ; yet the Divine Immanence must be taught in such a way as to assert at the same time the Divine Transcendence.[1] If not, God is identified with Nature. The notion of Immanence needs careful scrutiny as to the sense in which it is used—although to many just now it seems soothing, like "Mesopotamia." The question had better not be argued as between Immanence and Transcendence. Rather it is this. Is the power at the back of the phenomenal world alive, or is it dead ? On the mechanistic theory of evolution it is dead. The world is running down like a watch. As the spring unwinds, many outward changes may be noted ; but these have no more real significance than the changing positions of the hands of the watch. There is, in fact, no real change. All was fixed when the watch was made and wound. Nothing further of interest can happen. One event there is in this view in the life of the universe—the making and starting of the watch ; but that is all. We may describe its movements and analyse its works ; but neither God nor man can affect their action.

To the other view, the one changeless reality

[1] This seems to me the cardinal error of M. Loisy. In *L'Eglise et l'Evangile* he said with truth that the Creeds had been developed in an atmosphere of faith in the Divine Transcendence. But he seemed to desire a conformity to doctrines of Immanence which, instead of combining the two, would sacrifice altogether the Transcendence.

is the Love of God; and the world shows an ever present freedom. Part of its history may, for practical purposes, be expressed in mechanical categories. Such formulæ are never anything but abstract. Since the universe has a Living Will behind it, there occur at intervals new facts, real changes, free and strange occurrences. Some took place probably in the development of species, certainly in the life of man. Probably the animal world, certainly human life, is history, not mechanism. All attempts to set it out in deterministic formulæ are failures.

How far that freedom goes, we do not know. Certainly it does not mean that everything is possible. Freedom to man is the power to choose between alternatives, not to do anything he pleases. What is clear is this. If in the universe there exist a being or beings with wider knowledge and deeper powers than man, and if they can influence this world, they will probably do so in ways which we cannot understand; and they will by their action produce many disturbances beyond our power. Much evidence attests facts of that character. The capital instance is the cycle of stories that hangs about Jesus of Nazareth. Why are we to reject a view which is consonant with the theistic and personal interpretation of things, merely in obedience to a conception of nature which has become obsolete, and to a confusion of the scientific with the political sense of the terms "law and order"? The way is clearer, now that presuppositions are admittedly at the bottom of the negative opinion. Not that we have any right to complain of presuppositions; as M. Poincaré says, " We cannot do without them, even in the most " rigid scientific investigation." [1]

This is even more true in regard to the phenomena of a religion which claims to be a revelation. The moment we get beyond normal occurrences, the persuasive force of the evidence depends on our general view. Hume argued that the improbability of miracles is so great as to counterbalance all not merely actual, but any conceivable, evidence. This argument is valid, provided we know enough to be sure of that improbability. So long, however, as the world contains so much that is beyond us, we are justified in refusing to apply this criterion. Further considerations in favour of a probability on the other side have been stated above.

III. THE CRITICS AND THE NARRATIVES

" But," it is said, " you are ignoring the " argument from the documents. Is it not

[1] " On dit souvent qu'il faut expérimenter sans idée pré-" conçue. Cela n'est pas possible; non seulement ce serait " rendre toute expérience stérile, mais on le voudrait qu'on ne " le pourrait pas. Chacun porte en soi sa conception du monde " dont il ne peut se défaire si aisément." (La Science et l'hypothèse, p. 170.)

" the case that most of those who have ex-
" amined the evidence with the resources of
" modern scholarship have arrived at a negative
" conclusion in regard to the crucial miracles ? "
They have.   Nobody need be concerned to deny
Dr. Sanday's statement that the German critics,
as a body, though not universally, maintain the
view that these events did not take place ;
neither, in their judgment, did the Incarnation
take place.[1] Short work would be made by most
of them of anyone who, like the two Lady
Margaret Professors, desires to retain the
Nicene theology while rejecting these narratives.   Dr. Sanday declares that we know
more than we used to do of the workings of a
community mind ; consequently, stories like
those of the Virgin Birth and the Resurrection might have won credence in less
time than would be needful in a different
atmosphere.   This may be true ; but the same
principle affords us a criterion no less valuable
for judging the vaunted unanimity of the critics.
Is it not a fact that the atmosphere of continental criticism for the last century has been
unfavourable to the supernatural, and that
it is difficult, though not impossible, for a man
who holds by the traditional account to attain
reputation ? "We do not really believe in a Divine

[1] So they do, it now appears, of many other things, including the action of their own troops in Belgium. Professor
Moll of Berlin has disproved all this on the theory of group-
hypnotism.

" Christ at all ; all our criticism starts from a "position antagonistic," or words like this, were written some years ago in a letter to the writer which opened his eyes to the real bias of " scientific " criticism. The fact is that nearly all the negative critics start with the presupposition that whatever view they defend, it must not be that of the Christian tradition. The community of thought and feeling in which analytic criticism works is a very real community, though scattered in place. That community is no less unfavourable to faith in such an event as the Resurrection as the Early Church was favourable : and I see no reason to believe with modern professors that they must be right, and St. Peter and St. John wrong in their account of it. For the presuppositions of the early Christians were founded on a right and personal view of the world ; that of the Teutonic critics involves, though not always consciously, the mechanical conception.

One further point about the evidence may be noted. Among its strongest points are the victory of the Christian Church and its continued existence. Gibbon himself saw how strong was this argument, and tried to meet it in his famous five points ; but it never has been met. The case for the New Testament narrative is very different from what it would be if the events had left no issue. If Christianity were to die (*i.e.* miraculous Christianity), there would be grounds for disbelieving in the reality of these occurrences. It often seems like dying; but it strangely revives. If the experience of the past three centuries is of any value, what is more likely to die is that form of Christianity known as Liberalism. In practice it fades, first into Unitarianism, and then into unbelief.

Secondly, a right judgment of the New Testament experience depends on our view of it as a whole. Is there not ground for believing that here we are in the presence of a mighty inrush from the power behind the phenomenal world, producing a coruscation of wonders ? The more I read the New Testament, the more certain I am that this is the true interpretation of what the early Christians thought they were experiencing ; and, unless some other considerations inhibit me, I should suppose that what they thought was justified in fact. Such inhibition, as I have tried to show earlier, does not exist. Therefore I feel justified in holding that the experience is of that order best described as supernatural. If this be so, it is under the belief that the whole is a strange and miraculous occurrence that we analyse the particular items, and not *vice versâ*. It is the refusal, by the great majority of critics, even to consider such a claim that seems to me to make their work of such exiguous value as history.[1]

[1] Professor Bethune-Baker does appear to think we should treat the thing as a whole. It must not be supposed that this criticism applies only to heterodox writers ; some orthodox work is vitiated by this narrowly analytic method.

One modern man of science writes as follows :
" I am convinced that we cannot tear all the
" miracles from the New Testament, much less
" the cardinal miracles of the Resurrection of
" our Gospels, without creating a new set of
" difficulties, historical, intellectual, moral."
This position has been adopted by men of very
different sympathies from Sir William Barrett.
Critics of the academic centre are scornful of
the theories of Professor Drews, or Dr. Jen-
sen, or Mr. J. M. Robertson; yet they are
not to be ignored.   Some of them argue
with plausibility. Mr. Robertson, a convinced
rationalist, is so deeply persuaded of the integral
character of the Gospel miracles that he prefers
to cut the Gordian knot, and, rather than accept
them, to deny to our Lord every element of
historical reality. No one supposes that the
protagonists of liberalism have sympathy with
these attempts; yet they afford evidence of
the excesses to which rationalism is driven,
when carried to its logical extreme and resolved
to admit no evidence of Divine Revelation.[1]

[1] It may be well to cite two other statements of Sir William
Barrett, for they bear on the question of the general credibility
and range of the supernormal.

(a) " Miracle is essentially the direct control by mind of
" matter outside the organism ; in other words, a supernormal and
" incomprehensible manifestation of mind. As such, miracles
" did not cease with the Apostolic ages, but have continued
" down to the present time."

(b) " To deny miracles because of their incredibility is to
" deny the equally incredible but familiar phenomena of
" nutrition."

IV. GENERAL CONSIDERATIONS

Diverse are the causes which hinder us from accepting as authoritative the utterances of some distinguished critics.   One of these is the fact that their judgments never amount to more than plausible hypotheses for explaining part of the evidence ; although too often they are given out as certitudes.   This has been the case with some of the wilder hypotheses of M. Loisy, which he proclaims as facts.   Another is the prevalence of fashions in scholarship, and their frequent changes.   Even in matters like textual criticism, the recent work of Professor Clark on this subject is evidence of the uncertainty which still attaches to many of the judgments that seemed secure. On grounds of purely textual criticism and apart from all religious sympathy, Professor Clark would have us reverse our opinions on points so apparently settled as the priority of St. Mark, the non-authenticity of its conclusion, the story of the woman taken in adultery, and so forth. Professor Clark may or may not be right.   What he makes clear is that the received view is no more than a hypothesis, and not a very secure hypothesis.

Deeper, however, than this is men's distrust of the pontifical infallibility of criticism.   So far from thinking the critic more likely to be right than the Apostles, the plain Christian finds him devoid of some of the necessary quali-

T

ties of religious insight. Mr. Bernard Shaw
once made a gibe against University life in its
highest reaches as retaining the atmosphere
of the eighteenth century. This has a large
element of truth. The supreme facts of religious
experience are the tragedy of sin, the cry,
" What must I do to be saved ? ", the need of
uplifting, the desire for joy, its connection with
cross-bearing, above all the need of freedom—
" a God who can dance," in Nietzsche's phrase.
It has been well said, by one not a Christian,[1] that
the characteristic utterance of the religious
experience, whatever the dogma, is that of the
Psalmist, " Our soul is escaped like a bird out of
"the snare of the fowler ; the snare is broken
"and we are delivered." It is true. We have
escaped, and we are never more going to put our
feet in the trap. This feeling is in some men personal, in others social. All of it is without the
purview of academic critics debating the religious
problem on college bowling greens ; and this
is a fact of experience. For some years the
writer lived, however humbly, in the academic
world. That experience made two things apparent : (a) the importance of the contribution
of criticism ; (b) the fact that it is no more than
a contribution, one factor among many others,
all of which must be taken into account.

True, people are much in doubt about dogma
and facts ; but what they are in less doubt about
is the value of religion. It is not nearly so much

[1] Mr. F. M. Cornford, Fellow of Trinity.

the negative beliefs of liberalism as its attitude to
religious experience and to practical work that
arouses distrust of it.   Men feel that its atmosphere is not alluring, and its sympathies chill.[1]
The perpetual assumption of intellectual
superiority is not a winning attitude.   Until
the liberals can awaken general confidence as
to their retention of the values of the Christian life, they will speak, so far as concerns
the mass of Christians, to unregarding ears.
Meanwhile that retention of values does not
appear very likely.   Modernism, as professed
by Father Tyrrell or by William Scott Palmer,
did attempt to do that.   These thinkers had the
deepest reverence for the religious experience of
Christendom, and hoped to preserve all the
values—to sacrifice nothing of the tenderness
and the beauty enshrined in the prayers, the
worship, and the external cult, the historical
associations of the Church.   All this, however, is
treated with contempt by many liberals.   A
recent illuminating utterance on Modernism
seems to herald a yet more radical breach with
Christian living.[2]   Yet people are religious,
because they need these things.   If they feel no
need of them, they are at liberty to live, as

[1] Dr. Foakes-Jackson appears to have realised this, if we
may trust the account of a recent speech which he made at
the Churchmen's Union.

[2] "Post Modernism," by the Rev. J. M. Thompson, in the
Hibbert Journal for July 1914.   Still more valuable is the article
in the same number by the Dean of St. Paul's entitled "In-
stitutionalism and Mysticism."

many do to-day, a purely secular life with horizons bounded by the grave.

Here indeed is the issue. The protagonists of this school have spoken in language of dignity and reverence. No one would dream of treating their words with other than honour, or of denying their loyalty to the living Lord of Life and Death; but some doubt exists as to how far many other liberals would echo the words of Dr. Sanday in which he declares it "hypocritical" to say the Creeds with anything less than a "belief in the true Godhead of the "Father, Son, and Holy Ghost, and that our "Lord Jesus Christ is truly God and truly Lord, "very God and at the same time very man." Such a position is not easy to reconcile with such a passage as the following :

"The whole Universe, in all its several parts, reveals God, but this revelation is richer and more intense in human consciousness where specially gifted men such as prophets, poets, and philosophers reveal Him most of all. But I know of no fuller nor completer revelation of the Divine than that which is to be found in the life and character of Jesus. And as this revelation is of Supreme Love and Supreme Holiness, it may be considered final, and Christ's Personality as exceptional and unique. Only in this way can I think of Jesus as 'the only begotten Son of God.'"[1]

Certainly the plea for liberty, as it has been

[1] F. E. Powell, *With Eastern Merchandise*, p. 274.

argued, goes far beyond this ; it claims an entire freedom from all credal obligations.[1]

To one point neither of the two Lady Margaret Professors appears to have given sufficient attention, viz. the extreme difficulty of the doctrine of the Incarnation. To the writer, indeed, the Fatherhood of God is an article far more difficult of credit than any of the dogmas of ecclesiastical Christianity ; nor can I understand why one who has surmounted the obstacles to faith in God as Love and in our Lord as Incarnate should find much trouble in this miracle or in that, if they appear to be integral to the faith.

And, surely, they are integral. Is not the history of German and Genevan Protestantism, to which Dr. Sanday appeals, against him ? Has it not been proved more than once that, if the miraculous in Christianity be conceded, after a time Nicene doctrine follows in its wake ? It would not seem that such a course was inevitable ; but in practice it has been so. The Dean of Christ Church has recently shown how deeply the idea of the miraculous is involved in the Christian conception of God, and how, if we give up the

[1] It is interesting to quote another passage from this work :

"The idea associated with the principle of Nirvana—the ulti-"mate absorption of individual life into the ocean of quiescent "being—has always strongly appealed to me, and forms a feature "of the most rational mysticism" (*op. cit.*, p. 243).

Other indications can be found which show that even individual immortality is not safe, if some people have their way. *Personal Idealism and Mysticism*, by Dean Inge, will assist the reader to form a judgment.

one, we cannot hope for long to retain the other.[1]

Here, moreover, some can appeal to their own experience. We, who are unwilling to bow the knee to the new Baal, are not ignorant of his attractions; and some of us have passed through the fire.

From a personal knowledge one is able to state what has been the consequence of making these concessions, apparently so trifling. Speaking for the one person whose experience is certain to him, the writer can say this. For some time he gave up his belief in the Virgin Birth, or, to be accurate, he treated it as irrelevant; but he did not find it so. Slowly almost everything crumbled. Faith in the sacramental presence was not so much denied as practically forgotten. Harder and harder of credit became the great Christian doctrines —a dominant intellectualism seemed to cut away everything, not by argument, but by detaching faith from all living interest. Nothing indeed seemed to remain, except an unreasoning resolve to move the mind on. All meaning in life seemed to be vanishing; religion tended to become mere humanitarianism, for it is surely worth while to lighten people's lot, and to hang on to one's work, until the contrary is clear. All this is now expressed in a far more clear-cut fashion than it was lived; it is of tendencies, surmises, presuppositions rather

[1] See his pamphlet *The Miraculous in Gospels and Creeds*, especially the last page.

than of dogmatic statements that I speak. Yet all seemed to follow by a development, imperceptible but inevitable, living rather than logical from breathing that atmosphere, to which these apparently minor beliefs were akin.

Slowly change came. Penitence became real. After long years of struggle, pardon was sought in the sacrament of peace. Freedom, never given up as a belief, was seen to involve far more than had been thought. That notion of development which made miracles impossible was seen to be mechanical; the immanental philosophy was seen to be, if pushed to the extreme, a Pantheism identifying God and the world. So the glorious liberty of the children of God seemed given; and all the world grew younger day by day, as it does still. And may God never take from me, as I deserve, that grace so richly granted.

V. THE MODERN SPIRIT

What is most modern in the world to-day is the sense of freedom. If we are apt to hear with distrust the clamour of liberalism, it is because it seems to us to be so far from liberal in its general conception, and often to deny, alike to God and to man, that freedom which is the very essence of spiritual reality. This denial, it should be said, is by implication rather than by statement. It is because we feel it in our bones that we are apprehensive of the

chilling breath of mere liberalism, not because
we are ignorant of its arguments or insensitive
to its attractions. No religious movement has
much to offer to the sin-stained soul of men,
if its leaders—in place all but the highest—can
indulge in sneers at " those who purchase cheap
forgiveness by being washed in the blood of the
Lamb." There is more of true modernity in such
a book as Mr. James Stephens' *The Crock of Gold*,
innocent of any religious intention, than in the
taste which speaks of the convictions of fellow-
Christians as to the last things as "the brass band
of the Day of Judgment," or of the tyrannical
spirit which, in view of the revived faith in
freedom, "almost makes one wish back again
the iron hand of Victorian naturalism." [1]

Finally, it is urged that the Church should
become national. I wish she could. The aliena-
tion from the Church of the mass of working
men is a rebuke to the complacent Anglicanism
of cathedral closes, no less striking than the
detachment, by a rigid clerical and social conservatism, of many modern young women of education, repelled by convention. But can we
discern in this liberal movement any tendency
to close this breach ? On the contrary, it would
make it wider. It is the despised sacerdotalist
who has been going about preaching the gospel to
the poor, while the liberal has sat in his study,
sneering at his intellectual poverty. Even at
this moment we find leaders of this school much

[1] Inge, *The Church and the Age*, p. 11.

concerned with the defence of the plutocracy. One writes a pamphlet of which the only possible effect could be that of adding to the complacency of the comfortable classes. Another is ever vigilant against all forms of Christian Socialism. A third, yet more daring, hopes we may hear no more of winning the masses and tells us the working-man has not "a high survival value."

The last century has seen a revival in religion of almost unimaginable power from that condition of impotence to which Bishop Hoadly and his liberal compeers had reduced it. Foreign Missions have become a power which is beginning to react on Western Christianity; and that power is increasing. Little less wonderful have been the achievements of men like Father Lowder and Father Dolling in the slums. Worship has been made a reality; nor is it any longer a satire to speak of it as offered to the glory of God. The religious life has been revived. Only those who know the evils of great cities could say what we owe to the great sisterhoods; while for theology, Westcott has replaced Tillotson, and Liddon Blair. All this has not been the work of one party or of a few cliques; but it has been carried out upon the basis of these very beliefs which we are now invited to surrender. Knowledge of continental libraries; the occupation of pleasing academic or cathedral posts; an air of easy aloofness towards those who are bearing the burden and heat of the day (and are, by so doing, incidentally preserving these very

endowments)[1]—these things are not sufficient
to establish a claim on those for whom religion
is something more than an interesting topic of
discourse. It need not be said that this is not
true of all members of the school. Yet one of
its own spokesmen seemed dimly aware that
this liberal party had yet to win its spurs as a
religious power. So long as it considers devotion
waste of time, conversion rather vulgar, and self-
denial a foolish superstition, it may indeed win
literary honour; but it will not provide that
for which the world hungers—a religion which
shall satisfy the passion of the soul, bringing
forth from its treasure-house things new and old.
Modernism, if we are to use the word to denote
this complex of movements, is regarded with
unfavourable eyes on these grounds : that it is
not modern in spirit, but depends largely on a
view of things that is obsolete; that it is in fact
Victorian; that it is not liberal, but involves
notions inimical to spiritual freedom ; that it is
not popular, but aristocratic in its religious
sympathies ; not national, but academic; and
that its whole mental outlook, so far from being
broad, is restricted ;—while to the most potent
voices of the religious spirit it is deaf, and to
the visions of Eternal wonder it is blind.

[1] The Greville Memoirs and other first-hand authorities for
the period of the Reform Act make clear to every reader that
the Church was in imminent danger of Disendowment, and that
the changed attitude of the people was the direct result of
the great campaign in the poorer districts (of which men like
Father Lowder were the leaders) and of the revival wrought by
the Oxford Movement.

If the modernists should succeed for a couple of generations in establishing the claim of men like Tyrrell, and in preserving all the old values while broadening the basis, such success would not prove that they were right; but it would win them sympathy.   So far, they have failed to do this; and that failure has much to teach us !

On this subject the most important recent writings are as follows:

The Basis of Anglican Fellowship.   Bishop Gore.

The Miracle of Christianity.   Professor Bethune-Baker.

Bishop Gore's Challenge to Criticism.   Professor Sanday.

Restatement and Reunion.   Rev. H. B. Streeter.

An Open Letter in reply to Bishop Gore.   Professor Gwatkin.

Miracles in Modern Oxford Tracts.   By Rev. N. P. Williams.

The Miraculous in Gospels and Creeds.   The Dean of Christ Church.

The Bishop of Ely in the Preface to *The Gospels in the Light of Historical Criticism.*

The chapter on Miracles in Rev. T. J. Hardy's *The Religious Instinct.*[1]

---

[1] Mr. Hardy's chapter and Dean Strong's pamphlet, with Dr. Scott-Holland's notes, give perhaps the best statement of the case. Mr. N. P. Williams' tract on "Miracles" is closely reasoned, and in no way overstated; its author, however, seems to allow too little influence to the newer conceptions of nature which see evidences of freedom more generally. The same defect, it should be stated, applies to the writer's own chapter on "Freedom" in *The Gospel and Human Needs.* The general idea of the chapter, *i.e.* freedom, is not touched but more is allowed than need be to the older view that Nature as it is can be reduced to mathematical formulæ implying necessity.

Professor Scott-Holland's Notes on Dr. Sanday's pamphlet, reprinted from *The Commonwealth,* in the *English Church Review* for July 1914.

The Bishop of Winchester's Convocation speech reprinted.[1]

[1] Dr. Swete's valuable lecture, *The Ancient Creeds in Modern Life,*" should be added. No one can deny his eminence, even in these special studies which some of the minimisers think decisive. I quote two passages :

"No believer in the historical character of these two events will for a moment admit that they are in part or in whole *contra naturam,* or that any true miracle is such. There is, he will say, in this case, a supersession of the normal mode of the Divine working, and a consequent suspension of the normal mode, but not a contradiction. And he will ask himself whether, if such a departure from the normal mode can occur (*and to deny this is to deny the freedom of the Divine Will*), there was not an occasion for it when the Eternal Word was made man ; and when, being man, He became subject to death " (p. 24).

"The modern mind is averse from miracle, but it is still more resentful of that which it conceives to be a tampering with the plain meaning of words. It is not the miracles of the Conception and the Resurrection that constitute the ultimate difficulty in the way of this age when it is asked to accept the Christian faith. The difficulty lies further back, in the Incarnation itself. And the Incarnation is the very centre of the Faith. If you abandon it, you cut the heart out of the Creeds and of the Church herself.

"The Creeds, let it be plainly said, stand for a miraculous Christianity, because they stand for the truth of the Incarnation of the Eternal Word. . . . The Person of Christ is itself the miracle of miracles. No genuine re-interpretation of the Creeds can exclude miracle " (p. 29).

Printed by BALLANTYNE, HANSON & Co.
Edinburgh, Scotland

A SELECTION OF NEW BOOKS

OUR COMRADESHIP WITH THE BLESSED DEAD. By the Right Rev. J. P. MAUD, D.D., Bishop of Kensington. Fcap. 8vo. Paper cover, 1s. net ; cloth, gilt top, 2s. net.

NOTES ON THE PROPER PSALMS FOR HOLY DAYS. By the Right Rev. A. C. A. HALL, D.D., Bishop of Vermont. Crown 8vo, 2s. 6d. net.

THE WORK OF A GREAT PARISH. By Nine Portsea Men. Edited by the Rev. CYRIL F. GARBETT, Vicar, Hon. Canon of Winchester. With a Preface by THE ARCHBISHOP OF YORK. Crown 8vo, 5s. net.

THE FELLOWSHIP OF THE MYSTERY: Being the Paddock Lectures, 1913. By the Rev. JOHN NEVILLE FIGGIS, D.D., Litt.D. Crown 8vo, 5s. net.

WONDROUS LOVE: The Joy of Personal Devotion to Jesus. By the Rev. JESSE BRETT, L.Th., Chaplain of All Saints' Hospital, Eastbourne. With a Frontispiece. Crown 8vo, 3s. 6d. net.

THE RICHES OF THE HOUSE OF GOD: A Pilgrim's Quest in Pain and Joy. By FLORA ABIGAIL MACLEOD. With a Preface by the Rev. GEORGE CONGREVE, S.S.J.E. Crown 8vo, 2s. 6d. net.

THE PREPARATION FOR THE PASSION : A Study of the Incarnation and Virgin Birth of our Lord, and of His Life from Bethlehem to Cana of Galilee, including Notes on the First Five Chapters of St. Matthew and of St. Luke. By the Rev. JAMES S. STONE, D.D., Rector of St. James's Church, Chicago. Crown 8vo, 6s. net.

PRAYERS FOR THE CITY OF GOD. Arranged by GILBERT CLIVE BINYON, M.A. With Frontispiece. Fcap. 8vo, 2s. 6d. net.

IN THE FACE OF JESUS CHRIST: A Course of Meditations for the Christian Year. By the Rev. DAVID JENKS, Director of the Society of Sacred Mission, Kelham. 8vo, 6s. net.

THE FUNDAMENTALS OF THE RELIGIOUS STATE. By the Rev. SHIRLEY CARTER HUGHSON, Priest of the Order of the Holy Cross and Chaplain-General of the Community of St. Mary, Peekskill, New York. Crown 8vo, 6s. net.

THE SACRAMENTAL PRINCIPLE. By the Rev. PAUL B. BULL, M.A., of the Community of the Resurrection, Mirfield. Crown 8vo, 3s. 6d. net.

MY PRIESTHOOD: A Manual for the Clergy and for those looking towards Holy Orders. By the Rev. WALTER J. CAREY, M.A., Pusey House, Oxford. Crown 8vo, 3s. 6d. net.

LONGMANS, GREEN, AND CO.,

LONDON, NEW YORK, BOMBAY, CALCUTTA, AND MADRAS.

A SELECTION OF NEW BOOKS

THE LAYMAN'S LIBRARY.

Edited by F. C. BURKITT, F.B.A., Norrisian Professor of Divinity in the
University of Cambridge, and Rev. G. NEWSOM, M.A., Professor of
Pastoral Theology in King's College, London.

Crown 8vo, 2s. 6d. net each volume.

THE FAITH OF THE OLD TESTAMENT. By the Rev. ALEXANDER
NAIRNE, D.D., Canon of Chester. With a Preface by F. C. BURKITT,
M.A., F.B.A. [*Second Impression.*

SOME ALTERNATIVES TO JESUS CHRIST: A Comparative Study
of Faiths in Divine Incarnation. By JOHN LESLIE JOHNSTON, M.A.

WHAT IS THE GOSPEL? OR, REDEMPTION: A Study in the
Doctrine of Atonement. By the Rev. J. G. SIMPSON, D.D.

THE TEACHING OF CHRIST. An attempt to appreciate the main
lineaments of the Teaching of Christ in their historical proportion. By
the Rev. EDWARD GORDON SELWYN, M.A., Warden of Radley.

DISCOVERY AND REVELATION. By the Rev. HAROLD FRANCIS
HAMILTON, D.D., Professor of Pastoral Theology, Bishop's College,
Lennoxville, Canada, 1907-10.

Other Volumes of the Series are in Preparation.

THE CHURCH IN ROME IN THE FIRST CENTURY. Being the
Bampton Lectures for 1913. By the Rev. GEORGE EDMUNDSON, M.A.,
formerly Fellow of Brasenose College, Oxford. 8vo, 7s. 6d. net.

THE DEVELOPMENT OF ENGLISH THEOLOGY IN THE NINE-
TEENTH CENTURY (1800-1860). By the Rev. VERNON F. STORR,
M.A., Canon of Winchester. 8vo, 12s. 6d. net.

ENGLISH CHURCH LIFE FROM THE RESTORATION TO THE
TRACTARIAN MOVEMENT. Considered in some of its neglected or
forgotten features. By J. WICKHAM LEGG, Doctor of Letters (Honoris
Causa), Oxford. With Frontispiece. 8vo, 12s. 6d. net.

THE OFFERINGS MADE LIKE UNTO THE SON OF GOD. By
the Ven. WALTER STEPHEN MOULE, M.A., Principal of C.M.S. Training College, Ningpo, and Archdeacon in Chekiang, China. 8vo, 6s. net.

THE ONE CHRIST. An Enquiry into the Manner of the Incarnation.
By the Right Rev. FRANK WESTON, D.D., Bishop of Zanzibar. New
and Revised Edition. Crown 8vo, 6s. net.

THE LORD OF ALL GOOD LIFE: A Study of the Greatness of Jesus
and the Weakness of His Church. By DONALD HANKEY, Sergeant,
Rifle Brigade. Crown 8vo, 2s. 6d. net.

THOUGHTS FOR TEACHERS OF THE BIBLE. By the Very Rev.
J. ARMITAGE ROBINSON, D.D., Dean of Wells. Crown 8vo. Paper
cover, 6d. net ; cloth, 1s. net.

A SOWER WENT FORTH: Sermons Preached in the Chapel of the
Blessed Virgin Mary, Hardman Street, Liverpool. By the Rev. THOMAS
WILLIAM MAY LUND, M.A. Two volumes. Crown 8vo, 5s. net each.

LONGMANS, GEEEN, AND CO.,
LONDON, NEW YORK, BOMBAY, CALCUTTA, AND MADRAS.

17958